Down the Rotary Road

with

Judy Hopkins

That Patchwork Place

Acknowledgments

Special thanks are extended to:

Kathy Bungart, Terry Cerney, Debby Coates, Ann Corkran, Trish DeLong, Kay Dennis, Gail Engblom, Janet Gorton, Kathy Herring, Sarah Kaufman, Holly Layton, Clara Limberg, Emily McAlister, Dee Morrow, Doris Rhodes, Anne Richardson, Jennifer Roseland, Terri Shinn, Wendy Talbott, George Taylor, Stephanie Urda, Mary Jo Wenrick, and Janet Glen Wilson, for the fabulous quilts.

Peggy Hinchey, Ella Miller, Emma Smucker, and the Willing Workers Quilting Club, for their fine hand quilting.

Katherine Courtney, Debbie Caffrey, Judy Martin, Alice Berg, Mary Ellen Von Holt, and Sylvia Johnson, for sharing designs and inspiration.

Down the Rotary Road with Judy Hopkins

© 1996 by Judy Hopkins

That Patchwork Place, Inc.

PO Box 118

Bothell, WA 98041-0118 USA

Printed in Hong Kong

01 00 99 98 97 96   6 5 4 3 2 1

Library of Congress Cataloging-in-Publication Data

Hopkins, Judy,
    Down the rotary road / with Judy Hopkins,
        p.   cm.
    "30 sensational quilts from folk to fancy"—Cover.
    ISBN 1-56477-090-7
    1. Patchwork—Patterns. 2. Rotary cutting. 3. Machine quilting. 4. Patchwork quilts. I. Title.
TT835.H559   1996
746.46—dc20   95-46047
                                    CIP

Credits

Managing Editor .... Greg Sharp
Technical Editor .... Melissa Lowe
Copy Editor...................................... Liz McGehee
Proofreader...................................Melissa Riesland
Illustrator ....Laurel Strand
Illustration Assistant .... Lisa McKenney
Photographer .... Brent Kane
Photography Asssistant .... Richard Lipshay
Design Director.................................... Judy Petry
Text and Cover Designer.................. Amy Shayne
Production Assistant .... Claudia L'Heureux

MISSION STATEMENT

WE ARE DEDICATED TO PROVIDING QUALITY PRODUCTS AND SERVICES THAT INSPIRE CREATIVITY.

WE WORK TOGETHER TO ENRICH THE LIVES WE TOUCH.

That Patchwork Place is a financially responsible ESOP company.

Welcome!

I'm delighted you've decided to join me on this pleasant ramble down rotary road. It's an easy walk, with lots to see and do. Think of this as your guidebook—it's full of terrific traditional quilts, all rotary-cut and quick-pieced, and lots of other information that will help you on your way.

We start with tips on fabric selection and basic information about rotary cutting, machine piecing, and pressing your blocks and quilts. Be sure to familiarize yourself with the layered-strip approach we'll be using to make quick triangle units, as described on pages 11–12. This is my favorite quick-triangle method—it's fast, easy, produces very little waste, and lets me quickly stitch up "triangle squares" in dozens of different fabric combinations for those scrap-look quilts I love to make. In the back of the book, you'll find a wealth of general information on finishing your quilt, from squaring up blocks to adding a sleeve and label—and everything in between.

But the best part, of course, is the pattern section. I'm delighted with the richness and variety of the quilts my merry band of quiltmakers has put together. There are stunning two-fabric quilts, gorgeous "repeat-fabric" quilts, and sensational multi-fabric quilts in styles ranging from "folk" to "fancy." The projects are irresistible, and all are made with simple quick-cutting and -piecing techniques. I know you'll enjoy both the process and the product. Happy rambling!

Contents

FINISHING YOUR QUILT
95

QUILTING SUGGESTIONS
111

MEET THE AUTHOR
119

The Fabric Makes the Quilt!

When you make a quilt from a pattern book like this one, where the quilt's size, setting arrangement, and color scheme are specified, it's the fabrics you choose to work with that make your project personal and unique. I always encourage quilters to relax and trust their own judgment about fabric choices—but here are a few simple tips and hints to make the fabric-selection process easier.

Two-Fabric Quilts

Several of the quilts in this book are two-fabric quilts, such as the "Shaded Pinwheel" on page 20 and the "Bear's Paw" on page 39. The most important element in selecting fabric for a two-fabric quilt is contrast—the fabric used for the design must contrast strongly with the fabric used for the background. For maximum contrast, use solids, rather than prints, for two-fabric quilts. But don't rule out prints—even busy, multicolored prints will work if matched with low-key prints that "read" as solids. You'll know you have sufficient contrast if you can clearly see the "line" when patches of the two fabrics are joined.

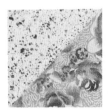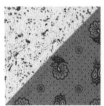

Make sure you can see the line where the two patches are joined.

Repeat-Fabric Quilts

For repeat-fabric quilts, such as "A Brighter Day" on page 85 and "Pinwheel Mosaic" on page 92, we use a coordinated group of fabrics and arrange them in a repetitive, predictable way. A wonderful multicolored print can cue the color scheme for a repeat-fabric quilt, whether or not that fabric is actually used in the quilt. Take into account the color proportion in the print that caught your eye. If your inspiration print is predominantly green and blue, with little accents of fuchsia, use greens and blues for the larger, more dominant pieces of your block or quilt and let the fuchsia play the same subordinate role that it does in the print. Neutrals (white, ivory, gray, black, or brown) can be added to any color scheme without changing it.

A key to interesting repeat-fabric quilts is textural variety. Prints come in distinct visual textures—large or small scale, open and airy or densely packed, curvy or linear. Try a plaid or stripe with a "garden-variety" calico, a large-scale floral with a small-scale, tone-on-tone print, or a polka dot with a paisley. Be a little adventurous—experiment with unusual prints and color combinations, and don't worry about cutting plaids on-grain or centering motifs.

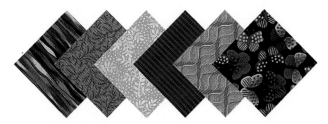

Use prints in a variety of visual textures.

Test your choices by making a trial block or a fabric paste-up before you buy and cut up yards of fabric.

Multi-fabric Quilts

In successful multi-fabric quilts, an abundance of fabrics and visual textures is balanced by a controlled, consistent placement of value or color within the blocks. When you are working with a large assortment of fabrics, decide on a value or color "recipe" and follow it consistently from block to block. This will define the pattern and unify the surface of the quilt.

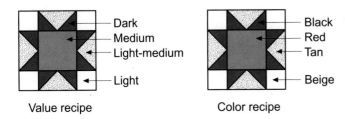

Value recipe — Dark, Medium, Light-medium, Light

Color recipe — Black, Red, Tan, Beige

Value defines the pattern in the multi-fabric "Anvil Star" on page 18. The small half-square triangles that make up the star points are cut from many different colors, but they are always the darkest fabric in the block. The small squares are assorted colors, but all are light in value.

In "Christmas Star" on page 48, color defines the pattern. Each of the blocks features a green and red Christmas Star design on a light gold background, but the blocks were made using several different green prints, several different red prints, and several different gold prints—a "run" of fabrics in each of the three color families. So, while the color arrangement is consistent, the fabric combinations vary from block to block.

The "Materials" sections for the multi-fabric quilt patterns in this book guide you toward certain value or color runs by specifying "a 2⅞" strip of each of 4 different dark prints" or "⅛ yd. each of 6 different green prints." When you're ready to buy or pull fabrics for a value-oriented run of dark prints, for example, you could choose dark prints all of the same color, such as all dark blues; dark prints similar in color, such as dark blues and purples; or dark prints of many colors, such as reds, blues, browns, and greens. For color runs, pick fabrics that you think work well together, but resist overmatching colors and give yourself a little latitude with value. Your six greens, for instance, could range from medium to dark and include avocado, emerald, forest, and teal. You could spice up the mix by adding a small amount of an adjacent color, such as blue, and/or a neutral, such as brown or black.

Value run of four darks (top).
Color run of six greens (bottom).

If you're working entirely from scraps or from yardage on hand, it may not be possible to follow your established value or color recipe in every block. If you're in a "use-it-up" frame of mind, just do the best you can with what you have and enjoy the results. Those scrappy, "make-do" quilts our grandmas made have a wonderful warmth and charm that many of us try to capture even when not driven by necessity!

Feel free to experiment and play as you plan and construct your multi-fabric quilt. Deliberately depart from the established color or value arrangement in one or two blocks. Make some blocks with high-contrast fabric combinations, using your lightest lights with your darkest darks, and others with low-contrast combinations. Use the wrong side of some of your fabrics. Cut plaids or stripes off-grain. If you make a piecing mistake, leave it in to add interest. To paraphrase fabric designer William Justema: "Repetition is what makes a pattern a pattern—but variation is what makes it rewarding to look at!"

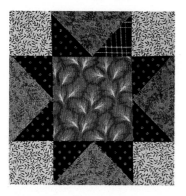

Repetition defines the pattern;
variation adds interest.

Fabric Content and Preparation

Most quilters prefer working with good-quality, lightweight, closely woven, 100% cotton fabrics—but it is not always possible to observe the "100% cotton rule" with quilts created from scraps or from fabric collections of long standing. While polyester content may make small patchwork pieces difficult to cut and sew accurately, I cheerfully include fabrics of uncertain content from my collection when the color or pattern seems appropriate for a particular quilt. Occasionally, I will even buy a blend, if it has unique color or design potential.

Wash all fabrics to preshrink, test for colorfastness, and get rid of excess dye. Use a mild soap and a short, cold-water cycle. Continue to wash fabric until the rinse water is completely clear. A cupful of vinegar in the rinse water may help set difficult dyes. Use a warm to hot dryer setting to dry fabrics. If you put a large towel in the dryer along with the fabric, there will be less twisting and tangling.

I wash fabrics as soon as I get home from the store, then I simply smooth and fold them when I take them out of the dryer. I press only those pieces that are impossibly wrinkled.

Rotary Basics

To make the quilts in this book, you'll need to know how to rotary-cut strips, squares, rectangles, and half- and quarter-square triangles. You'll also need to know how to make quick triangle units using the layered-strip method. Rotary-cutting equipment and the basic cuts are discussed below. The layered-strip method for quick half- and quarter-square triangle units is described on pages 11–12.

Equipment

You'll need a rotary cutter, a self-healing rotary-cutting mat, and two rotary-cutting guides marked in $\frac{1}{8}$" increments: a clear $\frac{1}{8}$"-thick ruler at least 22" long and a clear 6" or 8" cutting square.

Most quilters use the larger-sized rotary cutter with a blade about $1\frac{3}{4}$" in diameter. However, I find the smaller rotary cutter to be more manageable. An added advantage is that replacement blades for the small cutter cost less than blades for the large cutter, so one is not so slow to replace a dull blade.

You'll need an 18" x 24" cutting mat for cutting selvage-to-selvage strips from folded yardage and to cut large squares. I use a smaller mat when cutting small pieces of fabric and scraps.

There are many appropriate cutting guides on the market. Your long ruler should include lengthwise guidelines, some crosswise lines that run perpendicular to these strip-cutting guidelines, and markings for 45° angles.

My favorite cutting square is the Bias Square®, available in three sizes (4", 6", and 8") from That Patchwork Place. Although it was developed for a specialized purpose—cutting half-square triangle units from presewn bias strips—the Bias Square is an excellent general-purpose cutting guide. The markings and measurements are very easy to read, reducing the chances for error in measuring and cutting. The 8" Bias Square is large enough to accommodate quick-cutting requirements for almost any block, without being unwieldy.

Cutting

When rotary cutting, make straight, even cuts as close to the fabric grain as possible. Strips are usually cut along the crosswise grain. Squares and rectangles are cut on the lengthwise and crosswise grain. A slight variation from the grain is not a critical problem.

Refer to the illustration below. Lengthwise grain runs parallel to the selvage and has very little stretch. Crosswise grain runs from selvage to selvage and has some give to it. All other grains are considered bias. True bias is a grain line that runs at a 45° angle to the lengthwise and crosswise grains.

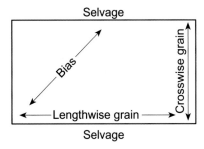

Hold your cutting guide firmly in place as you cut, keeping your fingers well away from the sharp rotary blade. Always roll the cutter away from your body! Start rolling the cutter before you reach the fabric edge and continue across the fabric, using firm, even pressure. Make sure that you have cut through all the fabric layers before you lift the cutting guide.

To straighten the fabric edge:

The first step in most rotary-cutting operations is to straighten the raw edge of the fabric.

1. Fold the fabric in half lengthwise, with selvages matching, and lay it on the cutting mat with the raw edge of the fabric to your left and the bulk of the fabric to your right (reverse these directions if you are left-handed). The fabric should lie flat and smooth on the mat; if it does not, refold and adjust the selvage edges until

there are no bubbles or bulges between the selvage edges and the fold.

2. Align the Bias Square with the fold of the fabric and place a long cutting guide firmly against it to the left.

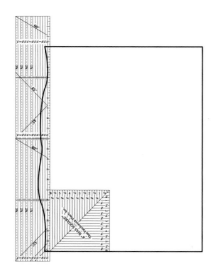

3. Remove the Bias Square and make a rotary cut along the right side of the long cutting guide.

To cut strips:

1. Align the required measurement on the long cutting guide with the straightened edge of the fabric and cut along the right-hand side of the long cutting guide. You can combine a Bias Square with the long cutting guide to make wider cuts. Open and check the fabric occasionally to make sure your cuts are straight. If the strips develop a "bend" in the middle, restraighten the fabric before cutting.

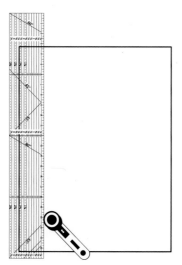

To cut squares and rectangles from strips:

1. Cut strips equal to the width specified in the pattern instructions (the dimensions given include 1/4"-wide seam allowances).

2. Without unfolding the strips, trim and straighten the selvage ends. Place the straightened ends toward the left side of the mat.

3. Align the required measurements on the Bias Square with the left and bottom edges of the strip and cut the fabric into squares or rectangles. Sometimes, you can get one or two additional pieces by unfolding the strip when you reach the folded right-hand edge.

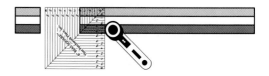

For some quilts, you will cut strips, join them into strip units, then cut pieces from the strip units. Trim and straighten one end of the strip unit, then align the required measurements on the Bias Square with the straightened end and cut.

To cut half-square triangles:

A half-square triangle is a right triangle with the short sides on the straight grain and the long side on the bias. A square, cut once diagonally, yields two half-square triangles.

1. Cut strips the required size, then cut the strips into squares as described on page 10.

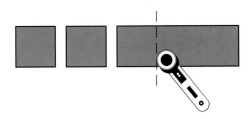

2. Line up the Bias Square diagonally across the squares, corner to corner, and cut.

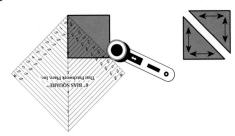

To cut quarter-square triangles:

A quarter-square triangle is a right triangle with the long side on the straight grain and the short sides on the bias. A square, cut twice diagonally, yields four quarter-square triangles.

1. Cut strips the required size, then cut the strips into squares as described on page 10.
2. Line up the Bias Square diagonally across the squares, corner to corner, and cut.
3. Without moving the resulting pieces, cut diagonally in the opposite direction.

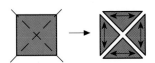

Making Quick Half-Square Triangle Units

Half-square triangle units typically consist of two contrasting triangles stitched together along the long edge to form a square as shown.

Every quilter has a favorite quick method for making these units. Some quilters draw and stitch grids, others cut and seam bias strips and then cut bias squares. The patterns in this book use an easy layered-strip technique that produces very little waste. Yardage and yield calculations are simple and straightforward, so they are more likely to be accurate. I think the technique is just as quick as methods that require premarking or strip stitching, and I love being able to make units in many different fabric combinations by combining short strip pieces.

To make half-square triangle units:

When multiple half-square triangle units are needed for a block or quilt, the pattern instructions will tell you to "Make ◩" from precut strips or strip segments.

1. Make strip pairs by layering contrasting strips or strip segments right sides together. When you are working with several fabrics in each color or value group, use as many different fabric combinations as possible, unless otherwise instructed. If you press the strip pairs after you align the fabrics, they will stick together, reducing the possibility of slippage during the cutting process and making it unnecessary to pin when you sew.

11

2. Cut squares from each layered pair of strips, using the measurements given in the pattern instructions.

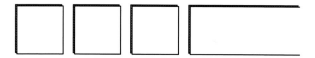

3. Cut the layered squares once diagonally from corner to corner.

4. Pick up and chain-piece the resulting triangle pairs along the long edges to make half-square triangle units; the pairs are matched and ready to sew. (See page 14 for a general description of chain piecing.) Cut the units apart and trim the corners before pressing.

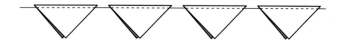

Making Quick Quarter-Square Triangle Units

Quarter-square triangle units typically consist of four contrasting triangles stitched together along the short edges to form a square as shown.

To make quarter-square triangle units:
1. Start by making half-square triangle units as described above, using the measurements given in the pattern instructions.

2. Cut the finished half-square triangle units once diagonally, perpendicular to the seam, and join the resulting pieces to make quarter-square triangle units.

  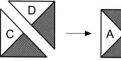

Note that two divided half-square triangle units will make two quarter-square triangle units, but you must mix and match the pieces cut from the half-square triangle units to make proper quarter-square triangle units.

Using Trimming Templates

Some quilt designs include squares that have one or more corners trimmed at a 45° angle, allowing you to add a triangle cut from a different fabric. The traditional Snowball block is an example.

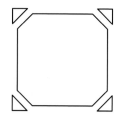 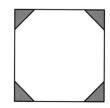

Corners trimmed
from square

Triangles added to
make Snowball block

In this book, a "trimming template" outline is provided with patterns that require these shapes. Carefully trace the outline onto stiff, clear plastic and cut out the shape. The outline is the correct size as given; never add seam allowances to a trimming template!

Cut the needed squares as described in the basic cutting instructions. Stack these in layers of four and place the trimming template in one corner, aligning the two short sides of the trimming template with the outside edges of the squares.

Hold the trimming template down firmly and push your Bias Square against the long edge of the template; the plastic will stop the cutting square at the proper position. Move the trimming template out of the way and cut along the square to remove the corner. Repeat for the other corners if instructed to do so.

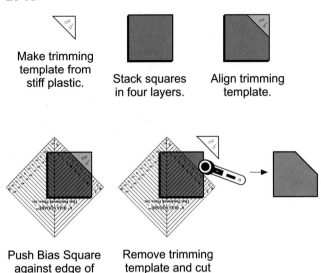

Make trimming template from stiff plastic.

Stack squares in four layers.

Align trimming template.

Push Bias Square against edge of trimming template.

Remove trimming template and cut along Bias Square.

An alternate method is to lay your Bias Square upside down over the appropriate trimming template outline, aligning the long side of the trimming template with the outside edge of the Bias Square. Then, outline the two short sides of the trimming template with masking tape on the underside of the Bias Square. You could also make a cutout from lightweight plastic or cardboard and tape it to the underside of the Bias Square. Align the edges of the masking tape or the cutout with the corner of your stack of squares; remove the corner by cutting along the edge of the Bias Square.

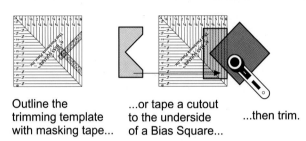

Outline the trimming template with masking tape...

...or tape a cutout to the underside of a Bias Square...

...then trim.

Some cutting guides, such as the ScrapMaster or the Rotary Mate™, may have edge markings in the size needed. If this is the case, the cutting guide is mentioned in the pattern instructions.

Machine Piecing

A well-maintained, straight-stitch sewing machine is adequate for most quiltmaking operations. If you are using a zigzag sewing machine, replace the zigzag throat plate with a plate that has a small, round hole for the needle to pass through, especially designed for straight stitching. If an even-feed ("walking") foot is available for your machine, it is worth buying one. You will find it invaluable for sewing on bindings and for straight-line machine quilting.

Use sewing-machine needles properly sized for cotton fabrics and change them frequently; dull or bent needles can snag and distort your fabric and can cause your machine to skip stitches. Set the stitch length at 10 to 12 stitches per inch. Make sure the tension is adjusted properly so you are producing smooth, even seams. I recommend using 100% cotton thread; I use a medium greenish-gray thread (the color you get when you mix all the Easter egg dyes together) for piecing all but the lightest and darkest fabrics.

Accurate cutting and piecing are critical elements of quiltmaking. Learn to machine stitch a straight, precise ¼"-wide seam. Find the ¼"-wide seam allowance on your machine by placing a Bias Square or a piece of accurate graph paper under the presser foot and lowering the needle onto the ¼" line. Place several layers of masking tape along the right-hand edge of the cutting square or graph paper to guide your fabric, making sure the tape does not interfere with the feed dogs.

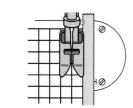

Put masking tape along edge
of graph paper to guide fabric.

Test your seam guide by cutting three short strips of fabric, each exactly 2" wide. Join the pieces into a strip unit, press the seams, and measure the finished width of the center strip. If you are sewing an accurate ¼"-wide seam, the center strip will measure exactly 1½".

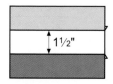

1½"

Seam 2" strips and measure the center.

You can save time and thread by chain piecing. Place the pieces that are to be joined right sides together with raw edges even; pin as necessary. Stitch the seam, guiding the pieces along the edge of your masking-tape guide, but do not lift the presser foot or cut the threads; just feed in the next set of pieces as close as possible to the last set. Sew as many seams as you can at one time; backstitching is not necessary. Clip the threads between the pieces either before or after pressing.

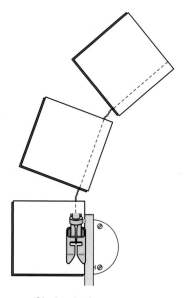

Chain piecing

Pressing

Most quilters avoid irons with an automatic shut-off feature but find that spray and shot-of-steam features are very useful. Treat yourself to an adjustable-height ironing board and keep your ironing equipment close to your sewing machine.

Be careful not to distort your pieces with heavy-handed ironing. Gently press every seam before attaching a new piece of fabric. Some quilters use a dry iron, while others prefer steam. I press seams open to make it easier to hand stitch the allover quilting patterns I frequently use for my quilts. However, the traditional quilters' rule is to press seams to one side, toward the darker fabric when possible. Side-pressed seams are stronger, and it is easier for most people to make corners meet properly when they can match opposing seams.

Snip or pull out threads that have been caught in the seams as you press; it is easier to tidy up the pieces when you are pressing the individual seams than to go back over the entire quilt later.

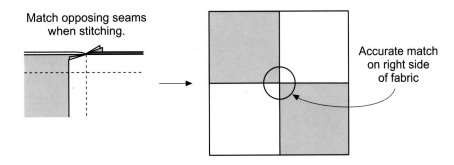

Match opposing seams when stitching.

Accurate match on right side of fabric

Appliqué

The appliquéd circles on "State Fair" (page 22) were made with the freezer-paper method described below. Freezer paper has a plastic coating on one side; you can fold the seam allowances over the freezer-paper edges and iron them to the plastic-coated side to make perfectly shaped appliqués with smooth edges.

Make a template from stiff plastic or cardboard. *Do not add seam allowances to the template.* Trace around the template on the plain side of a piece of freezer paper.

Cut out the freezer-paper shape on the pencil line. *Do not add seam allowances.* Pin the freezer-paper shape, plastic-coated side up, to the wrong side of the fabric. Cut the appliqué shape from the fabric, adding 1/4"-wide seam allowances around the outside edges of the freezer paper.

Add 1/4" seam allowance all around.

Using a hot, dry iron, carefully turn and press the seam allowance over the freezer-paper edges, easing in any excess fabric. Clip inside points and fold outside points.

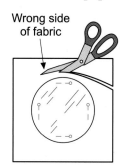

Press seam allowance over freezer-paper edges.

Iron the design in place onto the background fabric and appliqué the shape to the background, using thread that matches the appliqué piece. Catch just a few threads at the edge of the appliqué piece. Only a tiny stitch should show on the front of the quilt; the "traveling" is done on the back side.

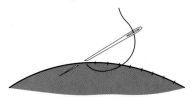

Appliqué stitch

After you have appliquéd the design, cut a small slit in the background fabric behind the appliqué. Cut away the background fabric, leaving a 1/4"-wide seam allowance all around, and carefully remove the freezer paper.

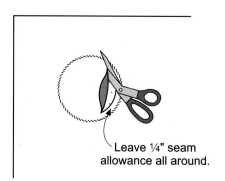

Leave 1/4" seam allowance all around.

Quilt Patterns

This section contains complete instructions for thirty rotary-cut quilts. Read the cutting and piecing directions for the quilt you plan to make before you begin. You may want to make a sample block to test the pattern and your fabric choices.

The finished quilt dimensions in the pattern instructions may differ from the dimensions given for the pictured quilts. The pattern dimensions are based on unquilted tops that are assumed to be cut and sewn with absolute precision. The dimensions of the pictured quilts reflect reality—the compounded effects of slight inaccuracies in cutting or piecing and any stretching or "take-up" that might have occurred during the quilting process. Special notations describe any other significant differences between the patterns and the pictured quilts.

The yardage requirements given in the "Materials" section should be adequate to complete the project if your fabric has been cut evenly from the bolt and does not shrink significantly when prewashed. Yardage calculations are based on 44"-wide fabric that has at least 42 usable inches of width after being preshrunk. If your preshrunk fabric is narrower than 42", you may need additional fabric. On the other hand, if your fabric is 42" or wider and you cut all the way to the end of a strip without counting the number of pieces cut, you may end up with a few pieces more than are actually needed to make a particular block or quilt.

Some of the yardage specifications include a parenthetical note, for example, "1 strip, 6⅞" x 42", each of 12 different light-medium prints, assorted colors, for blocks (Nearest cut is ¼ yd.)." The amount given in the parentheses is the nearest commercial cut. If you are using fabrics from your collection, cut selvage-to-selvage strips the specified width. If you need to purchase fabric, buy the yardage specified and cut the needed strips; use the remaining fabric for another project.

All cutting dimensions include ¼"-wide seam allowances. *Do not add seam allowances to the dimensions given in the cutting instructions.*

Cutting instructions for strips tell you to cut strips of a certain width and 42" long. Since 42" is the minimum length, it is fine if your strips are longer. Just cut selvage-to-selvage strips and proceed; don't trim the length to 42".

Cutting instructions for triangles indicate the size of the square from which you will cut the triangles. In the directions for half-square triangles, you are told to cut the squares "once diagonally"; for quarter-square triangles, you are told to cut "twice diagonally." If you need a refresher, see "Rotary Basics" on pages 9–13.

Half-Square Triangles   Quarter-Square Triangles
Cut once diagonally.   Cut twice diagonally.

Half- and quarter-square triangle units are made from layered strips. Basic instructions for this quick-triangle method appear on pages 11–12.

Use the photos that accompany the patterns as a reference while assembling your quilt. If you need to square up your blocks before assembling your quilt top, see "Squaring Up Blocks" on page 96. If you need help setting your blocks together with sashing or on point, see "Straight Sets" or "On-Point Sets," beginning on page 96.

See "Borders," beginning on page 100, for general information about bordering your quilt. Most of the projects in this book are completed with borders that have straight-cut corners, made from strips cut along the crosswise grain and seamed where extra length is needed. Purchase additional fabric if you want to cut these borders along the lengthwise grain.

General instructions for finishing your quilt—from marking quilting lines to adding a label—begin on page 102. Specific quilting suggestions for the quilts in this book begin on page 111.

ANVIL STAR

ANVIL STAR *by Ann Corkran, 1995, Anchorage, Alaska, 72" x 88".*
Clear pastels highlight this sentimental quilt. The anvil has a special meaning for Ann: her grandfather and great-grandfather were blacksmiths, and the one thing she has from their blacksmith shop is their anvil.

Dimensions:
72" x 88"

48 blocks, 8", set 6 across and 8 down; 2"-wide inner border, 10"-wide outer border.

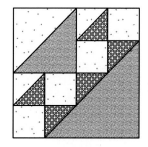

Anvil
8" block

Note: *Groups of 4 traditional Anvil blocks, set together in rotation, form the Anvil Star design.*

Materials: 44"-wide fabric

¼ yd. each of 12 different light prints, assorted colors, for blocks

1 strip, 6⅞" x 27", each of 12 different light-medium prints, assorted colors, for blocks (Nearest cut is ¼ yd.)

1 strip, 2⅞" x 33", each of 12 different dark-medium prints, assorted colors, for star points (Nearest cut is ⅛ yd.)

⅝ yd. light yellow print for seamed inner border

2⅛ yds. multicolored print for outer border

5⅓ yds. fabric for backing (lengthwise seam)

¾ yd. fabric for ⅜"-wide binding

Batting and thread to finish

Cutting:
All measurements include ¼" seams.

From *each* of the 12 light prints:
> Cut 1 strip, 2½" x 42", for a total of 12 strips. Cut each strip into 16 squares, 2½" x 2½", for a total of 192 squares.
> Cut 1 strip, 4⅞" x 11", for a total of 12 short strips.
> Cut 1 strip, 2⅞" x 13", for a total of 12 short strips.

From *each* of the 12 light-medium strips:
> Cut 2 squares, 6⅞" x 6⅞", for a total of 24 squares. Cut the squares once diagonally to make 48 half-square triangles.
> From the remaining piece of each strip, cut 1 strip, 4⅞" x 11", for a total of 12 short strips.

From *each* of the 12 dark-medium strips:
> Cut 6 squares, 2⅞" x 2⅞", for a total of 72 squares. Cut the squares once diagonally to make 144 half-square triangles.
> From the remaining piece of each strip, cut 1 strip, 2⅞" x 13", for a total of 12 short strips.

From the light yellow print:
> Cut 7 strips, 2½" x 42", for inner border.

From the *length* of the multicolored print:
> Cut 4 strips, 10½" wide, for outer border.

Directions

1. Make ◩: Layer the 2⅞" x 13" light and dark-medium strips, right sides together, to make 12 contrasting strip pairs. Cut 4 squares, 2⅞" x 2⅞", from each strip pair for a total of 48 layered squares. Cut the squares once diagonally and chain-piece the resulting triangle pairs to make 96 half-square triangle units.

2. Make ◩: Layer the 4⅞" x 11" light and light-medium strips, right sides together, to make 12 contrasting strip pairs. Cut 2 squares, 4⅞" x 4⅞", from each strip pair for a total of 24 layered squares. Cut the squares once diagonally and chain-piece the resulting triangle pairs to make 48 half-square triangle units.

3. Piece 48 Anvil blocks as shown. Combine the fabrics at random.

4. Set the blocks together in 8 rows of 6 as shown in the quilt photo, rotating every other block. Join the rows.

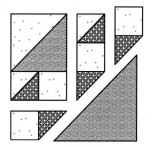

Make 48

5. Add the light yellow inner border and multicolored print outer border as shown in the quilt photo, seaming strips as necessary. See "Borders with Straight-Cut Corners" on page 100.

6. Layer with batting and backing; quilt or tie. See page 111 for a quilting suggestion. Bind with straight-grain or bias strips of fabric.

SHADED PINWHEEL

SHADED PINWHEEL *by Clara M. Limberg, 1995, Anchorage, Alaska, 43½" x 53½".*
Clara's eye-catching quilt combines a tone-on-tone black with a distinctive large-scale coral print.
Bull's-eye quilting provides a nice relief from the strong construction lines.

Shaded Pinwheel
10" block

Dimensions: 45" x 55"

12 blocks, 10", set 3 across and 4 down;
7½"-wide border.

Materials: 44"-wide fabric

⅞ yd. coral print for blocks
2 yds. tone-on-tone black print for blocks
    and border
3 yds. fabric for backing (crosswise seam)
½ yd. fabric for ⅜"-wide binding
Batting and thread to finish

Cutting:
All measurements include ¼" seams.

From the coral print:
Cut 2 strips, 3⅜" x 42". Cut the strips into a
    total of 24 squares, 3⅜" x 3⅜". Cut the
    squares once diagonally to make 48 half-
    square triangles.
Cut 7 strips, 3" x 42". Cut the strips into a to-
    tal of 48 seg-
    ments, each 5⅞"
    long, to make
    3" x 5⅞" rect-
    angles. Trim one
    corner of each
    rectangle at a
    45° angle exactly
    as shown.

Trim the corner
at a 45° angle.

From the black print:
Cut 7 strips, 3" x 42". Cut the strips into a
    total of 48 segments, each 5⅞" long, to
    make 3" x 5⅞" rectangles. Trim one

corner of each rectangle at a 45° angle as
shown. *Note that you are trimming a
different corner than you did from the coral
rectangles!*

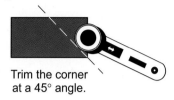

Trim the corner
at a 45° angle.

From the *length* of the remaining black print:
Cut 4 strips, 8" wide, for border.
Cut 2 strips, 3⅜" wide. Cut the strips into a
    total of 24 squares, 3⅜" x 3⅜". Cut the
    squares once diagonally to make 48 half-
    square triangles.

Directions

1. Join the 3⅜" black triangles
    to the trimmed coral rect-
    angles to make 48 units.

Make 48

2. Join the 3⅜" coral triangles
    to the trimmed black rect-
    angles to make 48 units.

Make 48

3. Join the units you made
    above to make 48 Shaded
    Pinwheel segments.

Make 48

4. Using the segments you made above, piece 12
    Shaded Pinwheel blocks as shown.
5. Set the blocks together in 4 rows of 3 as shown
    in the quilt photo; join the rows.
6. Add the black border as shown in the quilt
    photo. See "Borders with Straight-Cut Cor-
    ners" on page 100.
7. Layer with batting and backing; quilt or tie.
    See page 111 for a quilting suggestion. Bind
    with straight-grain or bias strips of fabric.

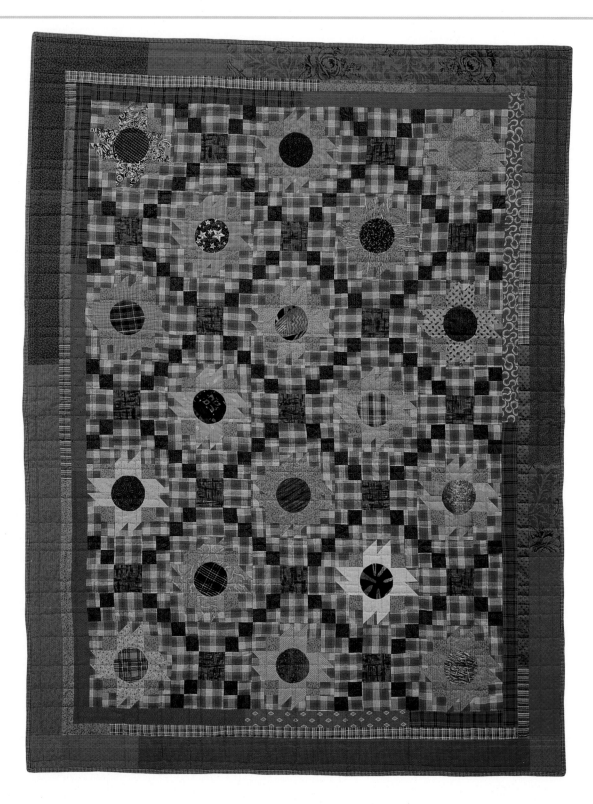

AUNT GOLDIE'S PRIZE WINNING QUILT *by Terri Shinn, 1995, Snohomish, Washington, 58" x 77¹/₂".*
Classic State Fair blocks, transformed into riotous sunflowers, are separated by alternate blocks that form a chain. Challenged to use just one fabric for the background of this quilt, Terri predictably opted for the unusual—a large-scale red-and-beige plaid. Note the collaged border treatment.

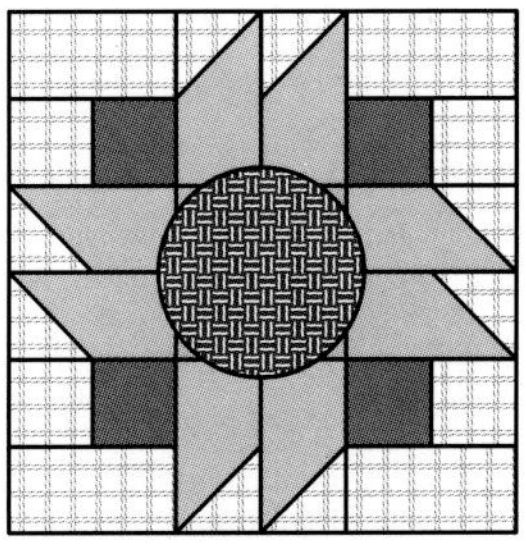

State Fair
9" block

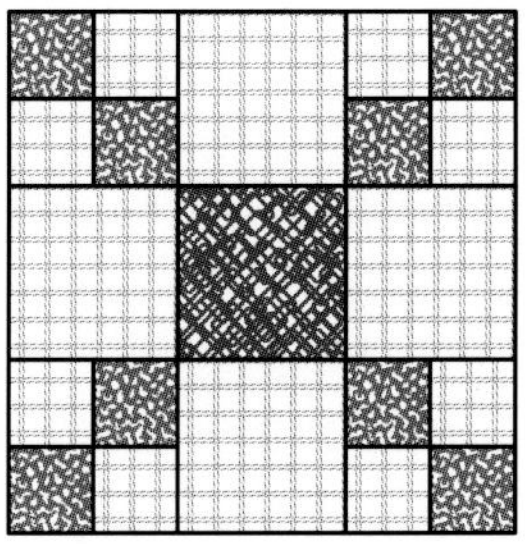

Chain
9" block

Dimensions: 60" x 78"

35 blocks (18 State Fair blocks and 17 Chain blocks), 9", set 5 across and 7 down; 2"-wide pieced inner border, 1½"-wide pieced middle border, 4"-wide pieced outer border.

Materials: 44"-wide fabric

¼ yd. brown print A for Chain block centers
½ yd. brown print B for Chain block
1 square, 4¼" x 4¼", each of 18 different dark prints for appliquéd circles
1 strip, 3⅞" x 21", each of 18 different gold and orange prints for State Fair blocks (Nearest cut is ⅛ yd.)
⅓ yd. green print for State Fair blocks
2⅛ yds. red plaid for background
1 strip, 2½" x 42", each of 7 different red prints and plaids for pieced inner border (Nearest cut is ⅛ yd.)
1 strip, 4½" x 42", each of 8 more red prints and plaids for pieced outer border (Nearest cut is ¼ yd.)*
1 strip, 2" x 42", each of 7 different green prints and plaids for pieced middle border (Nearest cut is ⅛ yd.)
3¾ yds. fabric for backing (crosswise seam)
⅝ yd. fabric for ⅜"-wide binding
Freezer paper
Batting and thread to finish

**Repeat some of the fabrics used for the inner border, if you wish.*

Cutting:

All measurements include ¼" seams.

From brown print A:
Cut 2 strips, 3½" x 42".

From brown print B:
Cut 7 strips, 2" x 42".

From *each* of the 18 gold and orange strips:
Cut 1 square, 3½" x 3½", for a total of 18 squares.
Cut each of the remaining pieces into 8 segments, each 2" wide, to make 2" x 3⅞" rectangles, for a total of 144 rectangles. Trim the corners of the rectangles at a 45° angle as shown.

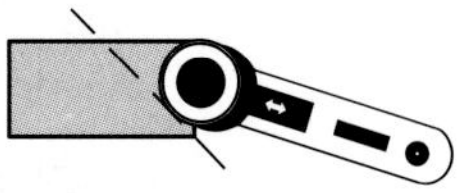

Trim the corner of each rectangle at a 45° angle.

From the green print:
Cut 4 strips, 2" x 42".

From the red plaid:
Cut 11 strips, 2" x 42".
Cut 5 strips, 2⅜" x 42". Cut the strips into a total of 72 squares, 2⅜" x 2⅜". Cut the squares once diagonally to make 144 half-square triangles.
Cut 11 strips, 3½" x 42". Cut 4 of the strips into a total of 72 segments, each 2" wide, to make 2" x 3½" rectangles. Cut 3 of the strips into a total of 34 squares, 3½" x 3½". Leave the remaining strips uncut.

Directions

1. Join 3½"-wide brown A strips and 3½"-wide red plaid strips to make 2 strip units as shown. Cut the strip units into a total of 17 segments, each 3½" wide.

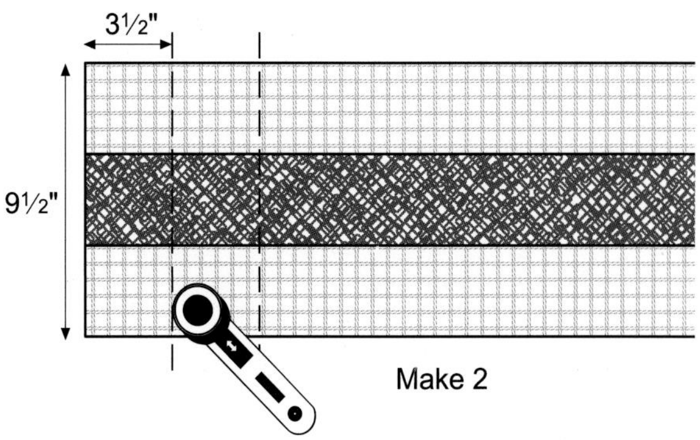

Make 2

2. Join 2"-wide brown B strips and 2"-wide red plaid strips to make 7 strip units as shown. Cut the strip units into a total of 136 segments, each 2" wide. Join the segments to make 68 four-patch units as shown.

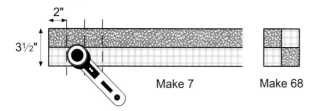

Make 7   Make 68

3. Join the four-patch units, the segments you cut in step 1, and the 3½" red plaid squares to make 17 Chain blocks as shown on page 23.

4. Join 2"-wide green strips and 2"-wide red plaid strips to make 4 strip units as shown. Cut the strip units into a total of 72 segments, each 2" wide. Add 2" x 3½" red plaid rectangles to each segment to make 72 units as shown.

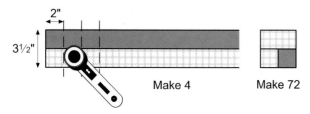

Make 4   Make 72

5. Join 2⅜" red plaid triangles to the trimmed gold and orange rectangles as shown. Join these units to make 72 pairs as shown. Use just one gold or orange fabric in each pair.

Make 144   Make 72

6. Using the units you made in steps 4 and 5 and the 3½" gold or orange squares, piece 18 State Fair blocks as shown. Match the gold or orange fabrics in each block.

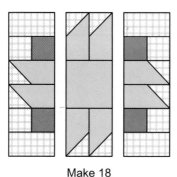

Make 18

7. Use the template below to make 18 freezer-paper circles. Pin the paper patches, plastic-coated side up, to the wrong sides of the 4¼" dark squares. Cut out circles, adding a ¼"-wide seam allowance. Turn and press the seam allowances over the edges of the paper patches and appliqué a circle to the center of each State Fair block as shown in the quilt photo. See "Appliqué" on page 16.

8. Set the blocks together in 7 rows of 5 as shown in the quilt photo, alternating State Fair and Chain blocks. Join the rows.

9. Cut the assorted 2½" x 42" red strips into various lengths and join them to make 4 pieced border strips, combining the fabrics at random. Repeat with the 2"-wide green strips and the 4½"-wide red strips. Add borders as shown in the quilt photo, trimming the strips as necessary. See "Borders with Straight-Cut Corners" on page 100.

10. Layer with batting and backing; quilt or tie. See page 111 for a quilting suggestion. Bind with straight-grain or bias strips of fabric.

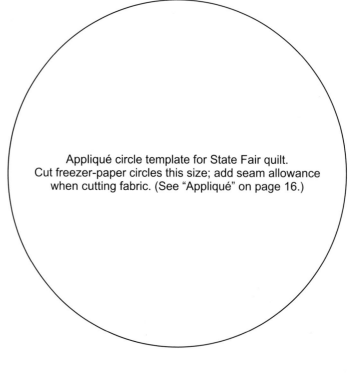

Appliqué circle template for State Fair quilt.
Cut freezer-paper circles this size; add seam allowance when cutting fabric. (See "Appliqué" on page 16.)

SNOWBALL STRIP

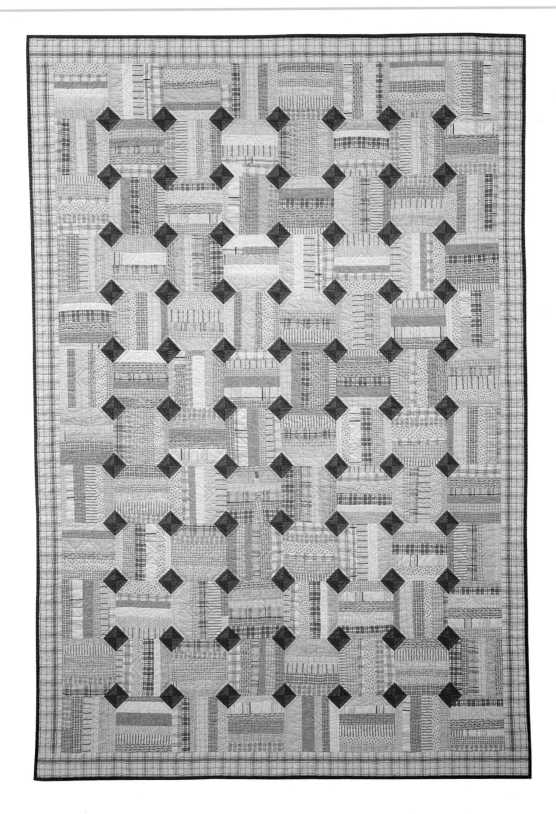

SNOWBALL STRIP *by Judy Dafoe Hopkins, 1995, Anchorage, Alaska, 66½" x 97".*
Blue and rust diamonds float on a scrappy concoction of light print strips, primarily plaids and stripes. Quilted
with perle cotton. This design would be great with black and white diamonds and hot, bright prints!

Dimensions:
68" x 98"

96 blocks, 7½", set 8 across and 12 down; 4"-wide border.

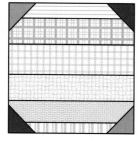

Snowball Strip
7½" block

Materials:
44"-wide fabric

⅜ to ½ yd. each of 20 different light blue and beige
   prints and plaids for blocks*
½ yd. blue solid for block corners
½ yd. rust solid for block corners
1¼ yds. blue-and-white plaid for seamed border
5⅞ yds. fabric for backing (lengthwise seam)
¾ yd. fabric for ⅜"-wide binding
Batting and thread to finish
ScrapMaster cutting guide (optional)

*If the fabric is cut evenly from the bolt and there is minimal shrink-
age when you prewash, ⅜ yd. will be adequate. You can use a mul-
titude of scrap strips 8 ½" or longer and of various widths instead of
purchased yardage.

Cutting:
All measurements include ¼" seams.

From each of the 20 light prints and plaids:
   Cut 1 strip, 2½" x 42".
   Cut 1 strip, 2¼" x 42".
   Cut 1 strip, 2" x 42".
   Cut 1 strip, 1¾" x 42".
   Cut 2 strips, 1½" x 42".
From the blue solid:
   Cut 5 strips, 2⅝" x 42". Cut the strips into a
      total of 77 squares, 2⅝" x 2⅝". Cut the
      squares once diagonally to make 154 half-
      square triangles.
From the rust solid:
   Cut 5 strips, 2⅝" x 42". Cut the strips into a
      total of 77 squares, 2⅝" x 2⅝". Cut the
      squares once diagonally to make 154 half-
      square triangles.
From the blue-and-white plaid:
   Cut 9 strips, 4½" x 42", for border.

Directions

1. Join the assorted light strips to make 20 strip
   units as shown. Each strip unit should contain
   6 strips: two 1½"-wide strips, one 1¾"-wide
   strip, one 2"-wide strip, one 2¼"-wide strip, and
   one 2½"-wide strip. Use many different fabric
   combinations and vary the placement of the
   strips according to width so each strip unit looks
   different.

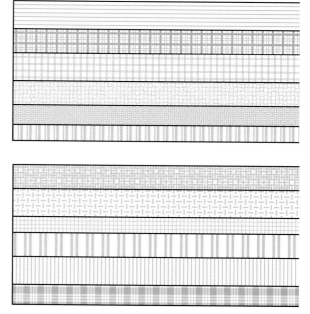

Make 20

2. Cut 5 squares, 8" x 8", from 19 of the strip units
   and 1 square from the remaining strip unit for
   a total of 96 squares. (The strip units may measure as much as 9" wide, raw edge to raw edge,
   when sewn. I allowed for extra width, as strip
   units sewn from many strips often don't end
   up as wide as we expect!)

3. Using the trimming template on page 27 or
   the 1⅞" "edge" markings on the ScrapMaster
   cutting guide, trim all 4 corners from 60 of the
   squares. (See "Using Trimming Templates" on
   page 12.) Add 2⅝" blue and rust corner triangles to make 30 Unit A and 30 Unit B as

shown. *Note that the strips all run horizontally and that the placement of the blues and rusts differs between Unit A and Unit B.*

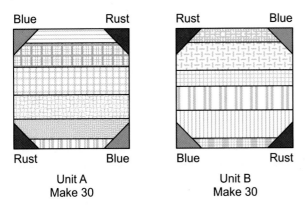

Blue   Rust

Rust   Blue

Unit A
Make 30

Rust   Blue

Blue   Rust

Unit B
Make 30

4. Trim 2 corners from 16 of the squares and add blue and rust corner triangles to make 6 Unit C and 10 Unit D for the outside edges of the quilt as shown. *Note that the strips all run horizontally.*

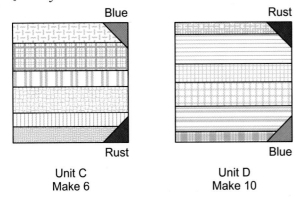

Blue

Rust

Unit C
Make 6

Rust

Blue

Unit D
Make 10

5. Trim 2 corners from 16 of the squares and add blue and rust corner triangles to make 6 Unit E and 10 Unit F for the outside edges of the quilt as shown. *Note that the strips all run vertically.*

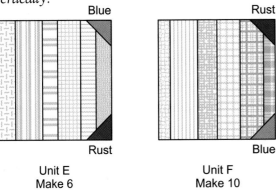

Blue

Rust

Unit E
Make 6

Rust

Blue

Unit F
Make 10

6. Trim 1 corner from each of the remaining 4 squares and add blue and rust corner triangles to make 2 Unit G and 2 Unit H for the corners of the quilt as shown. *Note that the strips all run vertically.*

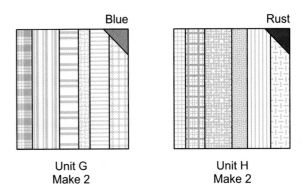

Blue

Rust

Unit G
Make 2

Unit H
Make 2

7. Set the blocks together in 12 rows of 8 as shown in the quilt photo, rotating the blocks as necessary to make the horizontal/vertical strip pattern. Join the rows.

8. Add the blue-and-white plaid border as shown in the quilt photo, seaming strips as necessary. See "Borders with Straight-Cut Corners" on page 100.

9. Layer with batting and backing; quilt or tie. See page 111 for a quilting suggestion. Bind with straight-grain or bias strips of fabric.

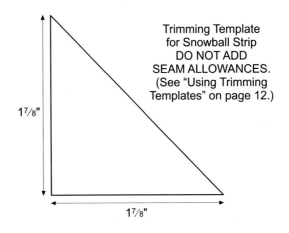

Trimming Template
for Snowball Strip
DO NOT ADD
SEAM ALLOWANCES.
(See "Using Trimming
Templates" on page 12.)

1⅞"

1⅞"

ARMY STAR

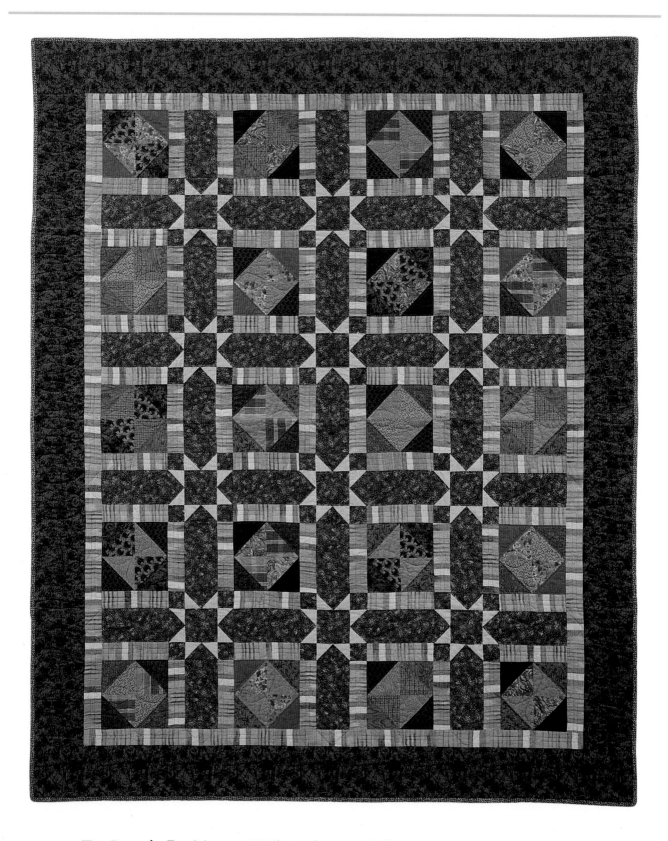

TOP BRASS *by Dee Morrow, 1995, Anchorage, Alaska, 71" x 85". Subtle stripes and sparkling stars grace this elegant quilt. Dee has deftly showcased a fine collection of green and plum prints.*

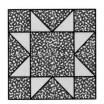
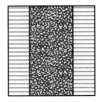
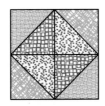

Block A
8" block

Block B
8" block

Block C
8" block

Dimensions: 72" x 88"

63 blocks (12 Block A, 31 Block B, and 20 Block C), 8", set 7 across and 9 down; 2"-wide inner border, 6"-wide outer border.

Materials: 44"-wide fabric

³/₈ yd. light yellow-green print for Block A

1⁷/₈ yds. purple print for Blocks A and B

1³/₄ yds. yellow-green stripe for Block B and seamed inner border

1 strip, 4⁷/₈" x 27", each of 8 different medium yellow-green prints for Block C (Nearest cut is ¹/₄ yd.)

1 strip, 4⁷/₈" x 27", each of 8 different medium-to-dark purple prints for Block C (Nearest cut is ¹/₄ yd.)

1⁵/₈ yds. dark purple print for seamed outer border

5¹/₃ yds. fabric for backing (lengthwise seam)

³/₄ yd. fabric for ³/₈"-wide binding

Batting and thread to finish

Cutting:
All measurements include ¹/₄" seams.

From the light yellow-green print:
Cut 4 strips, 2⁷/₈" x 42". Cut the strips into 48 squares, 2⁷/₈" x 2⁷/₈". Cut the squares once diagonally to make 96 half-square triangles.

From the purple print:
Cut 2 strips, 5¹/₄" x 42". Cut the strips into a total of 12 squares, 5¹/₄" x 5¹/₄". Cut the squares twice diagonally to make 48 quarter-square triangles.

Cut 10 strips, 4¹/₂" x 42". Cut 2 of the strips into a total of 12 squares, 4¹/₂" x 4¹/₂". Leave the remaining 8 strips uncut.

Cut 3 strips, 2¹/₂" x 42". Cut the strips into a total of 48 squares, 2¹/₂" x 2¹/₂".

From the yellow-green stripe:
Cut 24 strips, 2¹/₂" x 42", for Block B and inner border.

From the dark purple print:
Cut 8 strips, 6¹/₂" x 42", for outer border.

Directions

1. Join the light yellow-green and purple squares and triangles to make 12 Block A as shown.

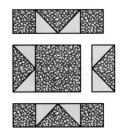

Make 12

2. Join 16 of the 2¹/₂"-wide yellow-green striped strips and the 4¹/₂"-wide purple strips to make 8 strip units as shown. Cut the strip units into a total of 31 segments, each 8¹/₂" wide, for Block B.

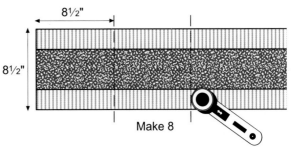

8¹/₂"

8¹/₂"

Make 8

3. Make ◢: Layer the 4⁷/₈" x 27" medium yellow-green and medium-to-dark purple strips, right sides together, to make 8 contrasting strip pairs. Cut 5 squares, 4⁷/₈" x 4⁷/₈", from each strip pair for a total of 40 layered squares. Cut the squares once diagonally and chain-piece the resulting triangle pairs to make 80 half-square triangle units.

4. Piece 20 Block C as shown above.

5. Set the blocks together in 9 rows of 7 as shown in the quilt photo; join the rows.

6. Add the yellow-green striped inner border and dark purple outer border as shown in the quilt photo, seaming strips as necessary. See "Borders with Straight-Cut Corners" on page 100.

7. Layer with batting and backing; quilt or tie. See page 112 for a quilting suggestion. Bind with straight-grain or bias strips of fabric.

SQUARES AND LADDERS

DON'T BUG ME *by Dee Morrow, 1994, Anchorage, Alaska, 62" x 82".*
Dee is definitely not afraid of orange—or bugs! Oversized sashing cut from a light-hearted, bug-infested
pictorial print anchors the sturdy squares and ladders. Quilted by Bobbi Moore.

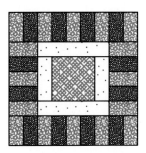

Squares and Ladders
13½" block

Dimensions: 64½" x 84"

12 blocks, 13½", set 3 across and 4 down with 6"-wide sashing and sashing squares; finished without a border.

Materials: 44"-wide fabric

2⅝ yds. light print for blocks and sashing pieces
½ yd. each of 3 different red-orange prints for blocks (Fabrics 1, 2, and 3)
⅝ yd. each of 3 different dark blue prints for blocks and sashing squares (Fabrics 4, 5, and 6)
5⅛ yds. fabric for backing (lengthwise seam)
⅝ yd. fabric for ⅜"-wide binding
Batting and thread to finish

Note: *For this project, you must have at least 42 usable inches of fabric after preshrinking. If the fabric is less than 44" wide on the bolt, you may need ⅜ yd. more of the light print and ⅛ yd. more of each of the red-orange and dark blue prints. Paste a snip of Fabrics 1–6 to a card and number the snips. Use this for reference during the cutting and assembly process.*

Cutting:
All measurements include ¼" seams.

From the light print:
Cut 8 strips, 2" x 42". Cut 3 of the strips into a total of 24 segments, each 5" wide, to make 2" x 5" rectangles. Cut the remaining strips into a total of 24 segments, each 8" wide, to make 2" x 8" rectangles.
Cut 11 strips, 6½" x 42". Cut the strips into a total of 31 segments, each 14" wide, to make 6½" x 14" rectangles for sashing pieces.

From the 3 red-orange prints:
Cut an 11" x 18" piece from one end of each fabric as shown. From each of these small pieces, cut 4 squares, 5" x 5", for a total of 12 squares.

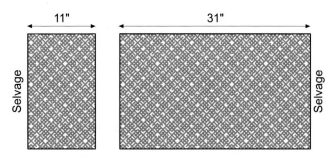

From each of the remaining 18" x 31" pieces, cut 8 strips, 2" x 31". Cut each strip in half for a total of 48 strips, 2" x 15½".

From the 3 dark blue prints:
Cut 1 strip, 6½" x 42", from each fabric for a total of 3 strips. Cut the strips into a total of 18 squares, 6½" x 6½", for sashing squares.
Cut an 11" x 16" piece from one end of each of the remaining 16" x 42" pieces, similar to the piece cut from the red-orange prints as shown above. Cut 1 square, 6½" x 6½", from each of 2 of these small pieces for sashing squares.
From each of the remaining 16" x 31" pieces, cut 6 strips, 2" x 31". Cut each strip in half for a total of 36 strips, 2" x 15½".

Directions

1. Join the 2" x 5" and 2" x 8" light rectangles to the 5" red-orange squares to make 12 units as shown.

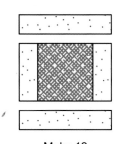

Make 12

2. Refer to your numbered fabric snips. Join 2" x 15½" strips of Fabric 1 and Fabric 4 to make 1 Strip Unit A and 1 Strip Unit B as shown. Strip Unit A uses 3 red-orange strips and 2 dark blue strips. Strip Unit B uses 5 red-orange strips and 4 dark blue strips. Cut each strip unit into 4 segments, each 3½" wide, for a total of 4 short segments and 4 long segments.

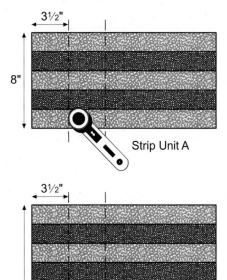

Strip Unit A

Strip Unit B

3. Repeat step 2, using Fabric 2 and Fabric 5 strips.
4. Repeat step 2, using Fabric 3 and Fabric 6 strips.
5. Repeat step 2, using Fabric 1 and Fabric 5 strips.
6. Repeat step 2, using Fabric 2 and Fabric 6 strips.
7. Repeat step 2, using Fabric 3 and Fabric 4 strips.
8. Piece 12 Squares and Ladders blocks as shown on page 31, matching the red-orange and dark blue strip-unit segments in each block.
9. Set the blocks together in 4 rows of 3 with the light print sashing strips and assorted dark blue sashing squares as shown in the quilt photo; join the rows. See "Straight Sets" on page 96.
10. Layer with batting and backing; quilt or tie. See page 112 for a quilting suggestion. Bind with straight-grain or bias strips of fabric.

GRANDPA'S DREAM *by Janet Glen Wilson, 1995, Girdwood, Alaska, 68" x 78". Janet has a special facility with the warm side of the color wheel. Note the unusual strip-pieced borders with corner squares. Quilted by Janet Glen Wilson and Jonnie Lazarus.*

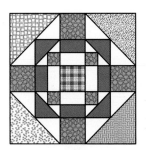

Harmony Square
12½" block

Dimensions: 67½" x 80"

20 blocks, 12½", set 4 across and 5 down;
2¼"-wide inner border, ¼"-wide second border,
1¼"-wide third border, 5"-wide outer border with
corner squares.

Materials: 44"-wide fabric

1⅝ yds. yellow print for block backgrounds and
  seamed second border
¼ yd. green plaid for block centers
1 strip, 5⅞" x 42", each of 6 different yellow-
  orange, gold, and green prints for block corners (Nearest cut is ¼ yd.)
1⅛ yds. rust print for blocks and seamed third
  border
2¾ yds. multicolored print for blocks, seamed inner and outer borders, and corner squares
4⅞ yds. fabric for backing (lengthwise seam)
⅝ yd. fabric for ⅜"-wide binding
Batting and thread to finish

Cutting:
All measurements include ¼" seams.

From the yellow print:
  Cut 7 strips, ¾" x 42", for second border.
  Cut 7 strips, 1¾" x 42".
  Cut 5 strips, 2⅛" x 42". Cut the strips into a
    total of 80 squares, 2⅛" x 2⅛". Cut the
    squares once diagonally to make 160 half-
    square triangles.
  Cut 7 strips, 3⅜" x 42". Cut the strips into a
    total of 80 squares, 3⅜" x 3⅜". Cut the
    squares once diagonally to make 160 half-
    square triangles.

From the green plaid:
  Cut 2 strips, 3" x 42".
**From *each* of the 6 yellow-orange, gold, and
green prints:**
  Cut 7 squares, 5⅞" x 5⅞", for a total of 42
    squares. Cut the squares once diagonally
    to make 84 half-square triangles. Four of
    these triangles will be extras.
From the rust print:
  Cut 14 strips, 1¾" x 42", for blocks and third
    border.
  Cut 4 strips, 3⅜" x 42". Cut the strips into a
    total of 40 squares, 3⅜" x 3⅜". Cut the
    squares once diagonally to make 80 half-
    square triangles.
From the multicolored print:
  Cut 7 strips, 3" x 42".
  Cut 4 strips, 1¾" x 42". Cut the strips into a
    total of 80 squares, 1¾" x 1¾".
  Cut 7 strips, 2¾" x 42", for inner border.
  Cut 7 strips, 5½" x 42", for outer border.
  Cut 1 strip, 9¼" x 42". Cut the strip into 4
    squares, 9¼" x 9¼", for border corners.

Directions

1. Join 4 each of the 3"-wide multicolored print
   strips, the 1¾"-wide rust strips, and the 1¾"-
   wide yellow strips with the two 3"-wide green
   plaid strips to make 2 strip units as shown. Cut
   the strip units into a total of 20 segments, each
   3" wide.

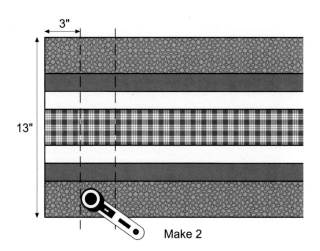

3"

13"

Make 2

2. Join 3 of the 1¾"-wide rust strips and the remaining 3"-wide multicolored and 1¾"-wide yellow strips to make 3 strip units as shown. Cut the strip units into a total of 40 segments, each 3" wide.

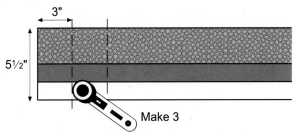

Make 3

3. Join the yellow triangles, the rust triangles, the small multicolored squares, and the yellow-orange, gold, and green triangles to make 80 units as shown.

Make 80

4. Piece 20 Harmony Square blocks as shown on page 34. Use 4 different prints for the outside corners of each block.

5. Set the blocks together in 5 rows of 4 as shown in the quilt photo; join the rows.

6. Piece the borders. Seam the yellow, rust, and multicolored border strips as needed to make 4 strips of each fabric, each about 65" long. Join these long strips to make 4 stripped border pieces as shown.

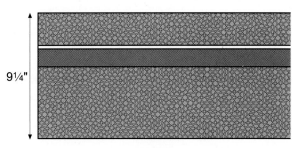

Make 4

7. Cut the border pieces to size and join to the quilt with the multicolored corner squares as shown in the quilt photo. See "Borders with Corner Squares" on page 101.

8. Layer with batting and backing; quilt or tie. See page 112 for a quilting suggestion. Bind with straight-grain or bias strips of fabric.

HOMEWARD BOUND TO UNION SQUARE

HALFWAY THERE *by Judy Dafoe Hopkins, 1994, Anchorage, Alaska, 45¹/₂" x 64".*
Classic Amish colors illuminate this two-block quilt. It's big enough to nap under, but small enough for the wall.
Quilted by Mrs. Ella Miller. (Collection of Andrew Seidlitz)

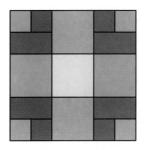

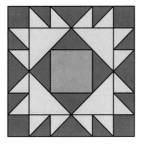

Homeward Bound
9" block

Union Square
9" block

Dimensions: 46" x 64"

15 blocks (8 Homeward Bound and 7 Union Square blocks), 9", set 3 across and 5 down; 1½"-wide inner border, 6"-wide middle border, 2"-wide outer border.

Materials: 44"-wide fabric

2 yds. black solid for block backgrounds and seamed middle border
1⅜ yds. turquoise solid for blocks and seamed inner and outer borders
¾ yd. blue solid for blocks
3 yds. fabric for backing (crosswise seam)
½ yd. fabric for ⅜"-wide binding
Batting and thread to finish

Cutting:
All measurements include ¼" seams.

From the black solid:
Cut 6 strips, 6½" x 42", for middle border.
Cut 8 strips, 2" x 42". Cut 2 of the strips into a total of 28 squares, 2" x 2". Leave the remaining strips uncut.
Cut 2 strips, 2⅜" x 42".
Cut 2 strips, 4¼" x 42". Cut the strips into a total of 14 squares, 4¼" x 4¼". Cut the squares twice diagonally to make 56 quarter-square triangles.

From the turquoise solid:
Cut 5 strips, 2" x 42", for inner border.
Cut 6 strips, 2½" x 42", for outer border.
Cut 1 strip, 3½" x 42".
Cut 2 strips, 3⅞" x 42". Cut the strips into a total of 14 squares, 3⅞" x 3⅞". Cut the squares once diagonally to make 28 half-square triangles.
Cut 4 strips, 2⅜" x 42". Cut 2 of the strips into a total of 28 squares, 2⅜" x 2⅜". Cut the squares once diagonally to make 56 half-square triangles. Leave the remaining strips uncut.

From the blue solid:
Cut 2 strips, 2" x 42".
Cut 5 strips, 3½" x 42". Cut 1 of the strips into 7 squares, 3½" x 3½". Leave the remaining strips uncut.

Directions

1. Join 2 of the 2"-wide black strips and the 2"-wide blue strips to make 2 strip units as shown. Cut the strip units into a total of 32 segments, each 2" wide.

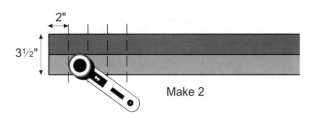

Make 2

2. Join the remaining 2"-wide black strips and 2 of the 3½"-wide blue strips to make 2 strip units as shown. Cut the strip units into a total of 16 segments, each 3½" wide.

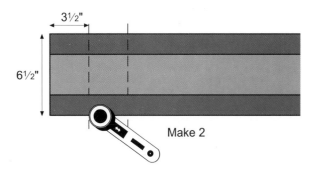

Make 2

3. Join the remaining 3½"-wide blue strips and the 3½"-wide turquoise strip to make 1 strip unit as shown. Cut the strip unit into 8 segments, each 3½" wide.

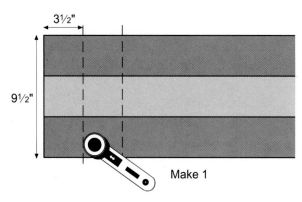

Make 1

4. Piece 8 Homeward Bound blocks as shown on page 37.

5. Make ◩: Layer the 2⅜"-wide black and turquoise strips, right sides together, to make 2 contrasting strip pairs. Cut 14 squares, 2⅜" x 2⅜", from each strip pair for a total of 28 layered squares. Cut the squares once diagonally and chain-piece the resulting triangle pairs to make 56 half-square triangle units.

6. Join the 3½" blue squares, the 4¼" black quarter-square triangles, and the 3⅞" turquoise half-square triangles to make 7 units as shown.

Make 7

7. Piece 7 Union Square blocks as shown.

Make 7

8. Set the blocks together in 5 rows of 3 as shown in the quilt photo, alternating Homeward Bound and Union Square blocks. Join the rows.

9. Add the turquoise inner border, black middle border, and turquoise outer border as shown in the quilt photo, seaming strips as necessary. See "Borders with Straight-Cut Corners" on page 100.

10. Layer with batting and backing; quilt or tie. See page 112 for a quilting suggestion. Bind with straight-grain or bias strips of fabric.

BEAR'S PAW

BRIAN'S BEAR PAW *by Kathleen Herring, 1993, Anchorage, Alaska, 72" x 92".*
Flannel-backed for warmth, this classic red-and-white quilt is used daily by Kathleen's six-year-old son.
The Sawtooth border adds a special touch. Quilted by Bobbi Moore.

Bear's Paw
14" block

Dimensions: *72" x 92"*

18 blocks (12 Bear's Paw blocks and 6 alternate blocks), 14", set on point; 2"-wide inner Sawtooth border, 4"-wide outer border.

Materials: *44"-wide fabric*

5²/₃ yds. ivory solid for blocks, alternate blocks, setting triangles, Sawtooth border, and outer border

1⁷/₈ yds. red solid for blocks and Sawtooth border

5⁵/₈ yds. fabric for backing (lengthwise seam)

³/₄ yd. fabric for ³/₈"-wide binding

Batting and thread to finish

Cutting:

All measurements include ¼" seams.

From the ivory solid:

Cut 12 strips, 2⁷/₈" x 42".

Cut 4 strips, 2¹/₂" x 42". Cut the strips into a total of 52 squares, 2¹/₂" x 2¹/₂". You need 48 of these squares for the blocks; use the remaining 4 squares for the corners of the Sawtooth border.

Cut 4 strips, 6¹/₂" x 42". Cut 2 of the strips into a total of 24 segments, 2¹/₂" wide, to make 2¹/₂" x 6¹/₂" rectangles. Leave the remaining 2 strips uncut.

Cut 3 strips, 14¹/₂" x 42". Cut the strips into a total of 6 squares, 14¹/₂" x 14¹/₂", for alternate blocks.

From the leftover pieces of the 14¹/₂"-wide strips, cut 2 squares, 11¹/₂" x 11¹/₂". Cut the squares once diagonally to make 4 half-square triangles for corner setting triangles.

From the *length* of the remaining piece of ivory solid, cut 4 strips, 4¹/₂" wide, for outer border.

From the remaining piece of ivory solid, cut 3 squares, 22¹/₂" x 22¹/₂". Cut the squares twice diagonally to make 12 quarter-square triangles for side setting triangles. There will be 2 triangles left over.

From the red solid:

Cut 12 strips, 2⁷/₈" x 42".

Cut 6 strips, 4¹/₂" x 42". Cut the strips into a total of 48 squares, 4¹/₂" x 4¹/₂".

Cut 1 strip, 2¹/₂" x 42".

Directions

1. Make ◸: Layer the 2⁷/₈"-wide ivory and red strips, right sides together, to make 12 contrasting strip pairs. Cut 14 squares, 2⁷/₈" x 2⁷/₈", from each strip pair for a total of 168 layered squares. Cut the squares once diagonally and chain-piece the resulting triangle pairs to make 336 half-square triangle units. You will use 192 units for the blocks and 140 units for the Sawtooth border, with 4 left over.

2. Join the 6¹/₂"-wide ivory strips and the 2¹/₂"-wide red strip to make 1 strip unit as shown. Cut the strip unit into 12 segments, each 2¹/₂" wide.

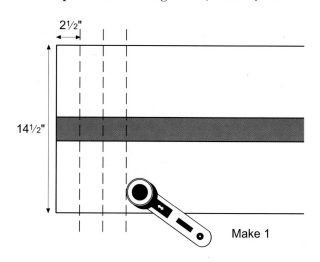

2½"

14½"

Make 1

3. Piece 12 Bear's Paw blocks as shown.

Make 12

4. Set the blocks together in diagonal rows with the ivory alternate blocks and the side and corner triangles. See "Assembling On-Point Quilts" on page 98. Join the rows as shown in the quilt photo. *Note that the setting triangles were cut large to allow some leeway in fitting the Sawtooth border to the quilt.*

5. Piece the Sawtooth border, using 40 half-square triangle units for each of the two long edges and 30 half-square triangle units for each of the two short edges. *Note that the Sawtooth units "turn" at the center of each pieced strip.* Add a 2½" ivory square to each end of the two short pieces. Measure the pieced border strips and trim the patterned center section of the quilt as necessary to make the border fit properly. Join the Sawtooth border to the quilt.

6. Add the ivory outer border as shown in the quilt photo. See "Borders with Straight-Cut Corners" on page 100.

7. Layer with batting and backing; quilt or tie. See page 113 for a quilting suggestion. Bind with straight-grain or bias strips of fabric.

STRING SQUARE

COSMIC OCEAN *by Gail Engblom, 1995, Anchorage, Alaska, 62" x 84".*
Add luscious contemporary batiks to a simple, old pattern and you get a blockbuster quilt—this one is
big enough for a twin-sized bed. Gail quilted it with perle cotton in a simple overall design.

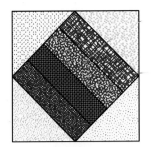

String Square
8½" block

Dimensions: 64" x 89½"

54 blocks, 8½", set 6 across and 9 down; 1½"-wide inner border, 5"-wide outer border.

Materials: 44"-wide fabric

⅛ yd. each of 18 different medium and/or dark blue and blue-green prints for blocks
⅓ yd. each of 7 different light and/or light-medium blue and blue-green prints for block corners
½ yd. aqua print for seamed inner border
1⅓ yds. multicolored print for seamed outer border
5⅜ yds. fabric for backing (lengthwise seam)
¾ yd. fabric for ⅜"-wide binding
Batting and thread to finish

Cutting:
All measurements include ¼" seams.

From *each* of the 18 medium and/or dark blue and blue-green prints
   Cut 2 strips, 2" x 42", for a total of 36 strips.
From *each* of the 7 light and/or light-medium blue and blue-green prints:
   Cut 2 strips, 5⅛" x 42", for a total of 14 strips. Cut 8 squares, 5⅛" x 5⅛", from each of 13 of the strips and 4 squares, 5⅛" x 5⅛", from the last strip for a total of 108 squares. Cut the squares once diagonally to make 216 half-square triangles.
From the aqua print:
   Cut 7 strips, 2" x 42", for inner border.
From the multicolored print:
   Cut 8 strips, 5½" x 42", for outer border.

Directions

1. Join the 2"-wide medium and/or dark blue and blue-green strips to make 9 strip units as shown. Combine the fabrics at random. Cut the strip units into a total of 54 segments, each 6½" wide.

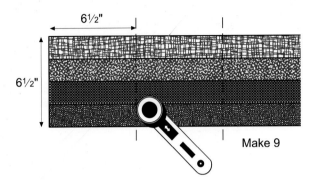

6½"

6½"

Make 9

2. Piece 54 String Square blocks as shown, combining the light and/or light-medium blue and blue-green half-square triangles at random.

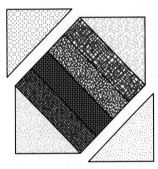

Make 54

3. Set the blocks together in 9 rows of 6 as shown in the quilt photo. *Note that the direction of the strips alternates from block to block.* Join the rows.
4. Add the aqua inner border and multicolored print outer border as shown in the quilt photo, seaming strips as necessary. See "Borders with Straight-Cut Corners" on page 100.
5. Layer with batting and backing; quilt or tie. See page 113 for a quilting suggestion. Bind with straight-grain or bias strips of fabric.

GAGGLE OF GEESE

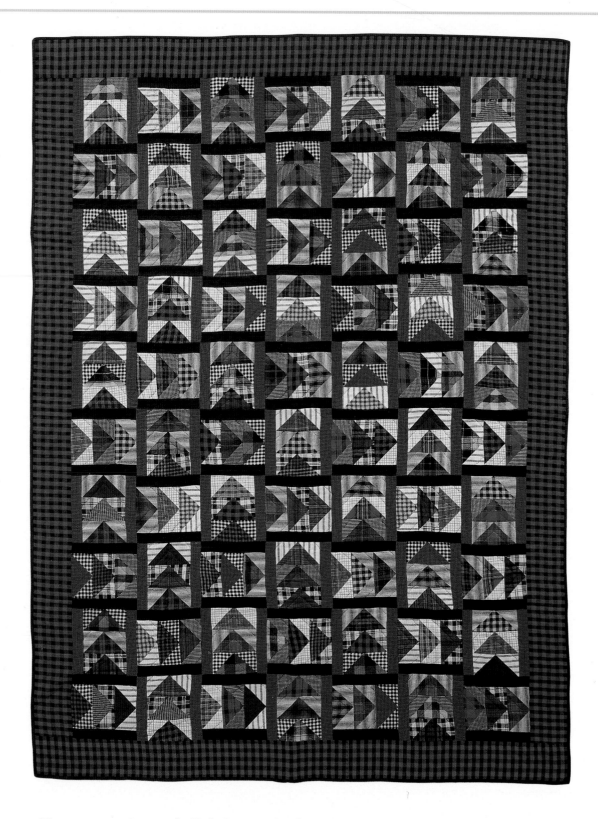

NORTHWOOD GAGGLE *by Deb Coates, 1995, Brush Prairie, Washington, 72" x 98½".*
Colorful and cozy, this flannel quilt has that great "lodge" look we all admire. Deb had to scramble to find
enough plaid flannels in the light value range. You may know the block as "Return of the Swallows."

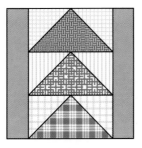

Block A
9" block

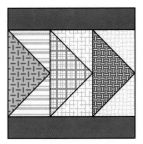

Block B
9" block

Dimensions: *73½" x 100½"*

70 blocks (35 Block A and 35 Block B), 9", set 7 across and 10 down; 5¼"-wide border.

Materials: *44"-wide fabric*

1/3 yd. each of 11 different light plaid flannels for block backgrounds*

1 piece, 7¼" x 16", each of 27 different dark plaid flannels (reds, blues, browns, golds, greens) for "geese" (Nearest cut is ¼ yd.)*

1⅛ yds. red flannel (a tiny check) for block edge strips

1⅛ yds. black flannel for block edge strips

1¾ yds. red-and-black checked flannel for seamed border

6 yds. fabric for backing (lengthwise seam)

¾ yd. fabric for ⅜"-wide binding

Batting and thread to finish

*Use the same fabric more than once, if you wish.

Cutting:

All measurements include ¼" seams.

From *each* of the 11 light plaid flannels:
　Cut 2 strips, 3⅞" x 42", for a total of 22 light strips. Cut the strips into a total of 210 squares, 3⅞" x 3⅞". Cut the squares once diagonally to make 420 half-square triangles.

From *each* of the 27 dark plaid flannels:
　Cut 2 squares, 7¼" x 7¼", for a total of 54 squares. Cut the squares twice diagonally to make 216 quarter-square triangles. Six of these will be extras.

From the red flannel:
　Cut 18 strips, 2" x 42". Cut the strips into a total of 70 rectangles, 2" x 9½"*.

From the black flannel:
　Cut 18 strips, 2" x 42". Cut the strips into a total of 70 rectangles, 2" x 9½"*.

*Your blocks may not measure exactly 9½" long when sewn. Cut these rectangles a little longer and trim to size after you piece the blocks, if you wish.

From the red-and-black checked flannel:
　Cut 10 strips, 5¾" x 42", for border.

Directions

1. Join the light plaid half-square triangles and the dark plaid quarter-square triangles to make 210 Flying Geese units as shown. Each unit uses 1 quarter-square triangle and 2 matching light plaid half-square triangles.

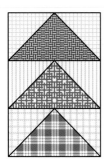

Make 210

2. Join the Flying Geese units into 70 groups of 3 as shown, combining the fabrics at random.

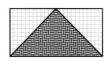

Make 70

3. Join 2"-wide red rectangles to each side of 35 units to make 35 Block A as shown above.

4. Join 2"-wide black rectangles to each side of the remaining units to make 35 Block B.

5. Set the blocks together in 10 rows of 7 as shown in the quilt photo; join the rows.

6. Add the red-and-black checked border as shown in the quilt photo, seaming strips as necessary. See "Borders with Straight-Cut Corners" on page 100.

7. Layer with batting and backing; quilt or tie. See page 113 for a quilting suggestion. Bind with straight-grain or bias strips of fabric.

THE COMET

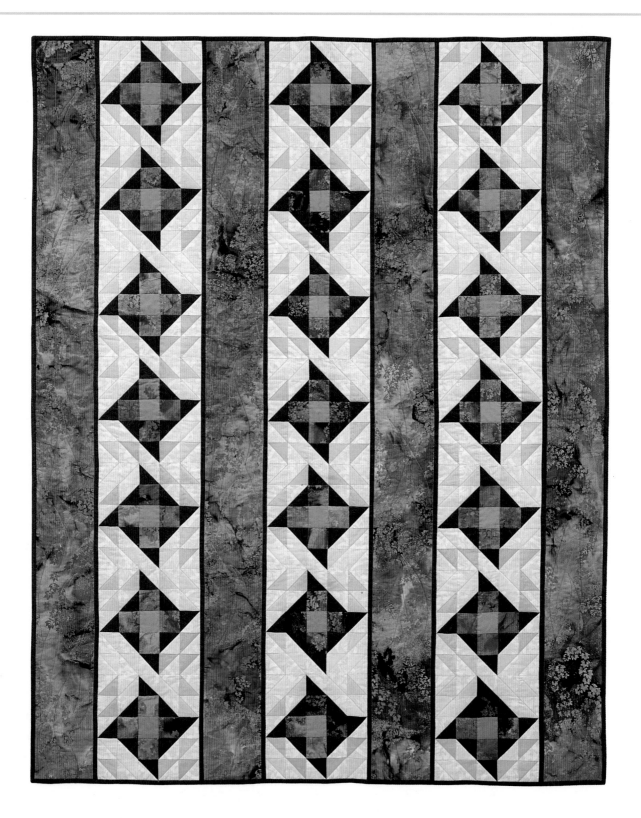

COMET *by George Taylor, 1995, Anchorage, Alaska, 54^1/$_4$" x 68^1/$_2$".*
The strippy set is a perfect foil for these delightful, whirling blocks. The triangle-studded background
features many different yellow and gold solids. George quilted an original flame motif in the batik bars.

Dimensions:
55" x 70"

21 blocks, 10", set in 3 vertical strips with ¹/₂"-wide edge strips; four 5¹/₂"-wide bars.

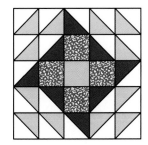

The Comet
10" block

Materials: 44"-wide fabric

1¹/₃ yds. ivory print for blocks
1 piece, 8" x 18", of bright gold solid for block centers (Nearest cut is ¹/₄ yd.)
1 strip, 2⁷/₈" x 42", each of 9 different yellow and gold solids for blocks (Nearest cut is ¹/₈ yd.)*
1 yd. dark blue print for blocks and seamed edge strips
2¹/₈ yds. multicolored print for blocks and bars
3¹/₂ yds. fabric for backing (crosswise seam)
⁵/₈ yd. fabric for ³/₈"-wide binding
Batting and thread to finish

*Use the same fabric more than once, if you wish.

Cutting:
All measurements include ¹/₄" seams.

From the ivory print:
   Cut 15 strips, 2⁷/₈" x 42".
From the bright gold solid:
   Cut 3 strips, 2¹/₂" x 18".
From the dark blue print:
   Cut 6 strips, 2⁷/₈" x 42".
   Cut 12 strips, 1" x 42", for edge strips.
From the *length* of the multicolored print:
   Cut 4 strips, 6" wide, for bars.
   From the remaining piece of multicolored print, cut 12 strips, 2¹/₂" x 18". Cut 6 of the strips into a total of 42 squares, 2¹/₂" x 2¹/₂". Leave the remaining strips uncut.

Directions

1. Make ◢: Layer the 2⁷/₈"-wide yellow and gold strips and 9 of the ivory strips, right sides together, to make 9 contrasting strip pairs. Cut 14 squares, 2⁷/₈" x 2⁷/₈", from each strip pair for a total of 126 layered squares. Cut the squares once diagonally and chain-piece the resulting triangle pairs to make 252 half-square triangle units.

2. Make ◢: Layer the 2⁷/₈"-wide dark blue strips and the remaining ivory strips, right sides together, to make 6 contrasting strip pairs. Cut 14 squares, 2⁷/₈" x 2⁷/₈", from each strip pair for a total of 84 layered squares. Cut the squares once diagonally and chain-piece the resulting triangle pairs to make 168 half-square triangle units.

3. Join the 2¹/₂" x 18" gold and multicolored print strips to make 3 short strip units as shown. Cut the strip units into a total of 21 segments, each 2¹/₂" wide.

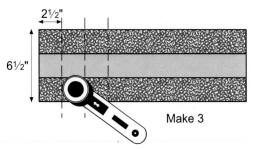

Make 3

4. Piece 21 Comet blocks as shown.

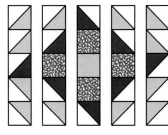

Make 21

5. Set the blocks together in 3 vertical rows of 7 blocks each as shown in the quilt photo.

6. Join the 1"-wide dark blue strips to the long sides of each row of blocks, seaming the strips as necessary.

7. Measure one of the rows of blocks at the center and cut the 6"-wide multicolored print strips to that measurement. Join the bars and the block strips as shown in the quilt photo.

8. Layer with batting and backing; quilt or tie. See page 113 for a quilting suggestion. Bind with straight-grain or bias strips of fabric.

CHRISTMAS STAR

CHRISTMAS STAR *by Judy Dafoe Hopkins, 1995, Anchorage, Alaska, 53³/₄" x 67¹/₄".*
This sparkling holiday quilt features a large assortment of red and green prints.
The striped inner border is a surprising—but pleasing—addition. Quilted by Mrs. Emma Smucker.

Dimensions:
54¾" x 67½"

*12 blocks, 12¾", set
3 across and 4 down;
¾"-wide inner border,
½"-wide middle border,
7"-wide outer border.*

Christmas Star
12¾" block

Materials: 44"-wide fabric

1 strip, 4¼" x 13", each of 12 different red prints
for blocks (Nearest cut is ⅛ yd.)
1 strip, 2⅜" x 21", each of 12 different green prints
for blocks (Nearest cut is ⅛ yd.)
¼ yd. each of 6 different light gold prints for blocks
⅞ yd. dark green print for block corners and
seamed middle border
2 yds. red print for block corners and outer border
¼ yd. tan/red/green stripe for seamed inner border
3½ yds. fabric for backing (crosswise seam)
1 yd. fabric for ¾"-wide binding (Cut 4¾"-wide
strips for ¾"-wide finished double-fold binding as shown in the quilt photo.)
Batting and thread to finish

Cutting:
All measurements include ¼" seams.

From *each* of the 12 red strips:
Cut 1 square, 4¼" x 4¼", for a total of 12
squares. Cut the squares twice diagonally
to make 48 quarter-square triangles.
Cut 1 square, 3½" x 3½", for a total of 12
squares.
Cut 4 squares, 1⁹⁄₁₆" x 1⁹⁄₁₆" (halfway between
the 1½" and 1⅝" marks on your cutting
square), for a total of 48 squares.

From *each* of the 12 green strips:
Cut 8 squares, 2⅜" x 2⅜", for a total of 96
squares. Cut the squares once diagonally
to make 192 half-square triangles.

From *each* of the 6 light gold prints:
Cut 1 strip, 2" x 42", for a total of 6 strips.
Cut 16 squares, 2" x 2", from each strip
for a total of 96 squares.

Cut 4 squares, 4¼" x 4¼", for a total of 24
squares. Cut the squares twice diagonally
to make 96 quarter-square triangles.
Cut 4 squares, 2¾" x 2¾", for a total of 24
squares. Cut the squares twice diagonally
to make 96 quarter-square triangles.

From the dark green print:
Cut 3 strips, 7¼" x 42". Cut the strips into a
total of 12 squares, 7¼" x 7¼". Cut the
squares once diagonally to make 24 half-
square triangles.
Cut 5 strips, 1" x 42", for middle border.

From the red print:
Cut 1 strip, 7¼" x 42". Cut the strip into 5
squares, 7¼" x 7¼". Cut the squares once
diagonally to make 10 half-square triangles.
From the *length* of the remaining piece of red
print, cut 4 strips, 7½" wide, for outer
border.
From the remaining piece of red print, cut 7
squares, 7¼" x 7¼". Cut the squares once
diagonally to make 14 half-square triangles.

From the tan/red/green stripe:
Cut 5 strips, 1¼" x 42", for inner border.

Directions

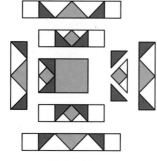

Make 12

1. Piece 12 Christmas
Stars as shown. Use
just 1 red print, 1
green print, and 1
light gold print in
each block.
2. Join the 7¼" red
and green triangles
to the stars as
shown above.
3. Set the blocks together in 4 rows of 3 as shown
in the quilt photo; join the rows.
4. Add the striped inner border, dark green middle
border, and red outer border as shown in the
quilt photo, seaming strips as necessary. See
"Borders with Straight-Cut Corners" on page
100.
5. Layer with batting and backing; quilt or tie.
See page 114 for a quilting suggestion. Bind
with straight-grain or bias strips of fabric.

LONDON ROADS

LONDON ROADS *by Stephanie Burrill Urda, 1995, Anchorage, Alaska, 47" x 59".*
Simple squares and strips and an abundance of prints combine to make this dynamic crib-sized quilt.
Try it in jelly-bean colors for an entirely different look.

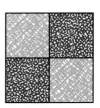

Block A
3" block

Block B
3" block

Block C
3" block

Dimensions: 49" x 61"

221 blocks (111 Block A, 56 Block B, and 54 Block C), 3", set 13 across and 17 down; 1"-wide inner border, 4"-wide outer border.

Materials: 44"-wide fabric

½ yd. each of 3 different ivory prints for Block A
⅞ yd. red print for Block A and seamed inner border
1 strip, 2" x 42", each of 6 different dark prints (greens, blues, and tans) for Block B (Nearest cut is ⅛ yd.)
1 strip, 2" x 42", each of 6 different medium prints (greens, blues, and tans) for Block B (Nearest cut is ⅛ yd.)
⅝ yd. navy blue print for Block C
⅞ yd. dark blue print for seamed outer border
3⅛ yds. fabric for backing (crosswise seam)
½ yd. fabric for ⅜"-wide binding
Batting and thread to finish

Cutting:
All measurements include ¼" seams.

From *each* of the 3 ivory prints:
Cut 8 strips, 1½" x 42", for a total of 24 strips.
From the red print:
Cut 17 strips, 1½" x 42", for blocks and inner border.
From the navy blue print:
Cut 5 strips, 3½" x 42". Cut the strips into a total of 54 squares, 3½" x 3½" (Block C).
From the dark blue print:
Cut 6 strips, 4½" x 42", for outer border.

Directions

1. Join the 1½"-wide ivory strips and 12 of the 1½"-wide red strips to make 12 strip units as shown. Use just one ivory print in each strip unit. Cut 9 segments, each 3½" wide, from each of 11 strip units. Then cut 12 segments, each 3½" wide, from the remaining strip unit. You will have a total of 111 segments (Block A). Use the remaining strip-unit pieces for another project.

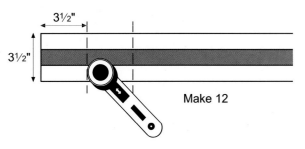

3½"

3½"

Make 12

2. Join the 2"-wide assorted dark and medium strips to make 6 strip units as shown. Cut the strip units into a total of 112 segments, each 2" wide.

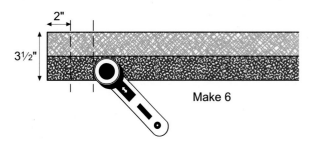

2"

3½"

Make 6

3. Piece 56 dark/medium Four Patch blocks (Block B), using matching segments in each Four Patch.
4. Set the blocks together in 17 rows of 13 as shown in the quilt photo; join the rows.
5. Add the red inner border and dark blue outer border as shown in the quilt photo, seaming strips as necessary. See "Borders with Straight-Cut Corners" on page 100.
6. Layer with batting and backing; quilt or tie. See page 114 for a quilting suggestion. Bind with straight-grain or bias strips of fabric.

SQUARES AND POINTS

SQUARES AND POINTS *by Sarah Kaufman, 1993, Shaw Island, Washington, 76" x 84".*
Sarah is a "salvage quilter" par excellence. For this star-spangled quilt, she combined contemporary prints,
authentic batiks, and years-old treasures from a remarkable scrap bag that predates The Beatles!

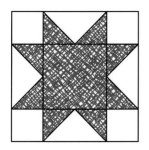

Squares and Points
8" block

Dimensions: 80" x 88"

90 blocks (45 Squares and Points blocks and 45 alternate blocks), 8", set 9 across and 10 down with half blocks and quarter blocks; finished without a border.

Materials: 44"-wide fabric

1 strip, 6½" x 33", each of 15 different gold and/or navy blue prints for blocks (Nearest cut is ¼ yd.)
⅝ yd. light gold print for half blocks
5¼ yds. ivory solid for background
7¼ yds. fabric for backing (2 crosswise seams), or use 2⅔ yds. of 90"-wide backing fabric
¾ yd. fabric for ⅜"-wide binding
Batting and thread to finish

Cutting:
All measurements include ¼" seams.

From *each* of the 15 gold and/or navy blue strips:
  Cut 3 squares, 4½" x 4½", for a total of 45 squares.
  From each of the remaining 6½" x 19½" pieces, cut 2 strips, 2⅞" x 19½", for a total of 30 strips. Cut 6 squares, 2⅞" x 2⅞", from each strip for a total of 180 squares. Cut the squares once diagonally to make 360 half-square triangles.

From the light gold print:
  Cut 4 strips, 2⅞" x 42". Cut 2 of the strips into a total of 19 squares, 2⅞" x 2⅞". Cut the squares once diagonally to make 38 half-square triangles. Leave the remaining strips uncut.
  Cut 3 strips, 2½" x 42". From one end of one of the strips, cut 2 squares, 2½" x 2½". Cut the remaining strip pieces into a total of 19 segments, each 4½" wide, to make 2½" x 4½" rectangles.

From the ivory solid:
  Cut 2 strips, 2⅞" x 42".
  Cut 14 strips, 2½" x 42". Cut the strips into a total of 220 squares, 2½" x 2½".
  Cut 1 strip, 4½" x 42". From this strip, cut 2 squares, 4½" x 4½", and 1 rectangle, 4½" x 8½".
  Cut 7 strips, 5¼" x 42". Cut the strips into a total of 50 squares, 5¼" x 5¼". Cut the squares twice diagonally to make 200 quarter-square triangles. One of these will be extra.
  Cut 12 strips, 8½" x 42". From each of 11 strips, cut 4 squares, 8½" x 8½", and 1 rectangle, 4½" x 8½", for a total of 44 squares (alternate blocks) and 11 rectangles. From the remaining strip, cut 1 square, 8½" x 8½", and 7 rectangles, 4½" x 8½".

Directions

1. Join the gold and/or navy blue squares and half-square triangles with 5¼" ivory quarter-square triangles and 2½" ivory squares to make 45 Squares and Points blocks as shown. Use just one gold or navy blue fabric in each block.

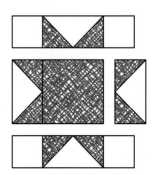

2. Make : Layer the 2⅞"-wide light gold and ivory strips, right sides together, to make 2 contrasting strip pairs. Cut 11 squares, 2⅞" x 2⅞", from each strip pair for a total of 22 layered squares. Cut the squares once diagonally and chain-piece the resulting triangle pairs to make 44 half-square triangle units. Two of these will be extras.

3. Piece 19 light gold and ivory half blocks and 2 light gold and ivory quarter blocks as shown.

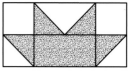

Make 19   Make 2

4. Set the blocks together in rows with the 8½" ivory alternate blocks, the half and quarter blocks, the 4½" x 8½" ivory rectangles, and the 4½" ivory squares as shown in the quilt photo. *Note that the pieced quarter blocks appear in just 2 of the quilt corners; the other 2 corners have plain ivory squares.*

5. Layer with batting and backing; quilt or tie. See page 114 for a quilting suggestion. Bind with straight-grain or bias strips of fabric.

ROLLING PINWHEEL

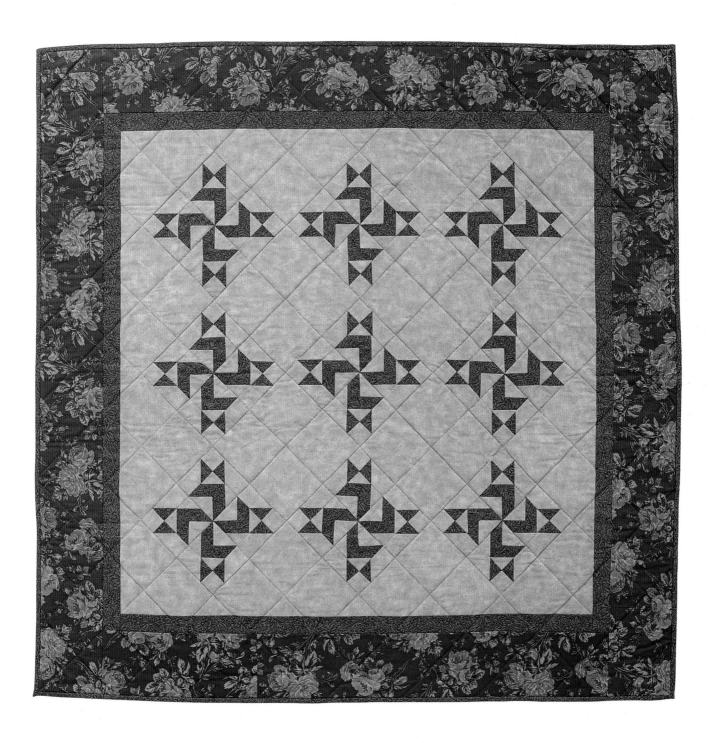

SPINNING IN TIME *by Jennifer Roseland, 1995, Anchorage, Alaska, 55" x 55".*
This delicate design demanded high-contrast, small-scale prints. The large-scale print used in the
border picks up the colors in the quilt and provides a pleasing textural counterpoint.

Rolling Pinwheel
9" block

Dimensions: 55¾" x 55¾"

13 blocks (9 Rolling Pinwheel and 4 alternate blocks), 9", set on point with 1¾"-wide "float"; 1½"-wide inner border, 5½"-wide outer border.

Materials: 44"-wide fabric

2 yds. pink print for background
⅞ yd. blue-green print for blocks and seamed inner border
1⅛ yds. multicolored floral print for seamed outer border
3½ yds. fabric for backing (lengthwise or crosswise seam)
½ yd. fabric for ⅜"-wide binding
Batting and thread to finish

Cutting:
All measurements include ¼" seams.

From the pink print:
  Cut 2 strips, 2" x 42". Cut the strips into a total of 36 squares, 2" x 2".
  Cut 3 strips, 2⅜" x 42". Cut the strips into a total of 36 squares, 2⅜" x 2⅜". Cut the squares once diagonally to make 72 half-square triangles.
  Cut 1 strip, 4¼" x 42". Cut the strip into 9 squares, 4¼" x 4¼". Cut the squares twice diagonally to make 36 quarter-square triangles.
  Cut 2 strips, 7¼" x 42". Cut the strips into a total of 36 segments, each 2" wide, to make 2" x 7¼" rectangles. Trim the

corners of the rectangles at a 45° angle as shown.

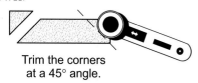

Trim the corners
at a 45° angle.

  Cut 1 strip, 9½" x 42". Cut the strip into 4 squares, 9½" x 9½", for alternate blocks.
  Cut 1 strip, 19" x 42". Cut the strip into 2 squares, 19" x 19". Cut the squares twice diagonally to make 8 side setting triangles. These pieces are cut extra large to allow for "float."
  Cut 2 squares, 9¾" x 9¾". Cut the squares once diagonally to make 4 corner setting triangles. These pieces are cut extra large to allow for float.
From the blue-green print:
  Cut 5 strips, 2⅜" x 42". Cut the strips into a total of 72 squares, 2⅜" x 2⅜". Cut the squares once diagonally to make 144 half-square triangles.
  Cut 1 strip, 4¼" x 42". Cut the strip into 9 squares, 4¼" x 4¼". Cut the squares twice diagonally to make 36 quarter-square triangles.
  Cut 5 strips, 2" x 42", for inner border.
From the multicolored floral print:
  Cut 6 strips, 6" x 42", for outer border.

Directions

1. Join 2⅜" half-square triangles and 4¼" quarter-square triangles to make 36 units with pink corners and 36 units with blue-green corners as shown.

Make 36   Make 36

2. Join the units you made in step 1 to make 36 units as shown.

Make 36

3. Join 72 blue-green half-square triangles to the 36 trimmed pink rectangles.

4. Piece 9 Rolling Pinwheel blocks as shown.

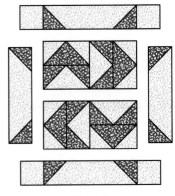

Make 9

5. Set the Rolling Pinwheel blocks and the pink alternate blocks and setting pieces together in diagonal rows as shown in the quilt photo. Join the rows. Trim the outside edges and square up the corners of the quilt as necessary, leaving 2" of fabric outside the block corners to allow the blocks to float. See "Assembling On-Point Quilts" on page 98.

6. Add the blue-green inner border and multi-colored floral outer border as shown in the quilt photo, seaming strips as necessary. See "Borders with Straight-Cut Corners" on page 100.

7. Layer with batting and backing; quilt or tie. See page 114 for a quilting suggestion. Bind with straight-grain or bias strips of fabric.

NINEPATCH PLAID

STRAWBERRY PATCH *by Janet Strait Gorton, 1994, Anchorage, Alaska, 55½" x 74".*
The large-scale floral print lends this easy Ninepatch quilt an extraordinary appeal. Janet's version is colored
for Christmas but would be a delight to doze under any time of year. Quilted by Mary Miller.

The strip-piecing method used in this pattern will yield enough pieces to make 41 or 42 blocks, several more than are needed to make the pictured quilt. The directions are written for 35 blocks; cut more segments and make more blocks, if you wish. You could use these blocks to make the quilt one row wider or longer than the one shown. The border fabric requirements given will accommodate a larger quilt.

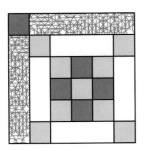

Ninepatch Plaid
9" block

Dimensions: 57½" x 75½"

35 blocks, 9", set 5 across and 7 down with 1½"-wide right and bottom edge sashing; 1"-wide inner border, 4½"-wide outer border.

Note: *The pictured quilt appears to have sashing with red corner squares, but those pieces actually are a part of the block, except for the pieces that finish the right and bottom edges.*

Materials: 44"-wide fabric

1⅝ yds. white-on-white print for blocks and seamed inner border
1⅛ yds. medium gray-green print for blocks
¾ yd. red print for blocks and sashing
2⅓ yds. multicolored floral print for blocks, sashing, and seamed outer border
3⅝ yds. fabric for backing (crosswise seam)
⅝ yd. fabric for ⅜"-wide binding
Batting and thread to finish

Cutting:
All measurements include ¼" seams.

From the white-on-white print:
Cut 8 strips, 5" x 42". Cut 4 of the strips into a total of 70 segments, each 2" wide, to make 2" x 5" rectangles. Leave the remaining strips uncut.
Cut 8 strips, 1½" x 42", for inner border.
From the medium gray-green print:
Cut 18 strips, 2" x 42".
From the red print:
Cut 11 strips, 2" x 42".
Cut 1 square, 2" x 2" (cut from scraps or from the end of one of the strips).
From the multicolored floral print:
Cut 5 strips, 8" x 42". Cut 2 of the strips into a total of 35 segments, each 2" wide, to make 2" x 8" rectangles. Leave the remaining strips uncut.
Cut 8 strips, 5" x 42", for outer border.

Directions

1. Join 8 of the 2"-wide gray-green strips and 4 of the 2"-wide red strips to make 4 strip units as shown. Cut the strip units into a total of 70 segments, each 2" wide.

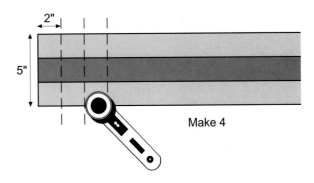

Make 4

2. Join 4 of the 2"-wide red strips and 2 of the 2"-wide gray-green strips to make 2 strip units as

shown. Cut the strip units into a total of 35 segments, each 2" wide.

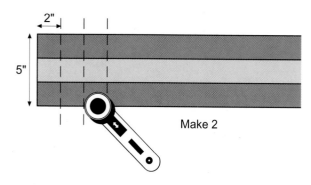

Make 2

3. Piece 35 red/green ninepatch units as shown.

Make 35

4. Join the remaining 2"-wide gray-green strips and the 5"-wide white-on-white strips to make 4 strip units as shown. Cut the strip units into a total of 70 segments, each 2" wide.

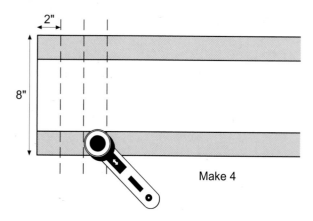

Make 4

5. Join the remaining 2"-wide red strips and the 8"-wide multicolored floral strips to make 3 strip units as shown. Cut the strip units into a total of 47 segments, each 2" wide. You will need 35 of these segments for the blocks. The

remaining 12 segments will be used to complete the right and bottom edge sashing.

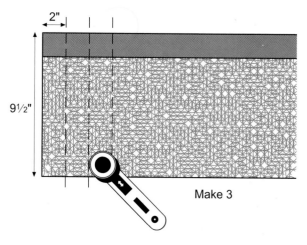

Make 3

6. Piece 35 Ninepatch Plaid blocks as shown.

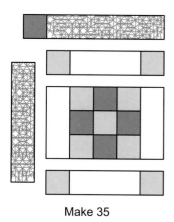

Make 35

7. Set the blocks together in 7 rows of 5 as shown in the quilt photo; join the rows.
8. Using the segments remaining from step 5 and the 2" red square, piece and add the right and bottom edge sashings as shown in the quilt photo.
9. Add the white-on-white inner border and multicolored floral outer border as shown in the quilt photo, seaming strips as necessary. See "Borders with Straight-Cut Corners" on page 100.
10. Layer with batting and backing; quilt or tie. See page 115 for a quilting suggestion. Bind with straight-grain or bias strips of fabric.

HOLLY'S HOUSES

HOLLY'S HOUSES by Holly Rebekah Layton, 1994, Anchorage, Alaska, 29½" x 27½".
Rows of inviting little houses, done up in plaids and stripes, nestle in a fairy-tale forest.
What a wonderful quilt for a child's room—or your own!

Little Quilts by Alice Berg, Mary Ellen Von Holt, and Sylvia Johnson (That Patchwork Place, Inc.) features a 5" x 5" version of this House block, made entirely from strips, in a number of appealing projects.

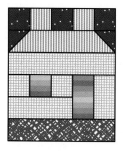

House
5" x 6" block

Dimensions: 30½" x 28"

12 blocks, 5" x 6", set 4 across and 3 down with ½"-wide sashing; 4"-wide border.

Materials: 44"-wide fabric

1 strip, 6" x 42", of black star print for sky (Nearest cut is ¼ yd.)

1 strip, 5½" x 42", of gray stripe for roofs and chimneys (Nearest cut is ¼ yd.)

¼ yd. gray-and-blue plaid for houses

⅓ yd. blue stripe for doors, windows, and sashing

⅛ yd. dark gray print for grass or gravel

⅔ yd. black tree print for border (directional fabric)

1 yd. fabric for backing

⅜ yd. fabric for ⅜"-wide binding

Batting and thread to finish

Cutting:
All measurements include ¼" seams.

From the black star print:
   Cut 2 strips, 1½" x 42". Cut the strips into a total of 36 squares, 1½" x 1½".
   Cut 1 strip, 1⅞" x 42". Cut the strip into 12 squares, 1⅞" x 1⅞". Cut the squares once diagonally to make 24 half-square triangles.

From the gray stripe:
   Cut 3 strips, 1½" x 42". Cut 1 of the strips into 24 squares, 1½" x 1½".
   Cut the remaining strips into a total of 12 segments, each 6¼" wide, to make 1½" x 6¼" rectangles. Trim the corners of the rectangles at a 45° angle as shown.

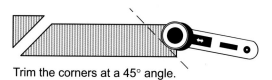

Trim the corners at a 45° angle.

From the gray-and-blue plaid:
   Cut 5 strips, 1½" x 42". Cut 2 of the strips into a total of 12 segments, each 5½" wide, to make 1½" x 5½" rectangles. Cut 1 of the strips into 12 segments, each 3½" wide, to make 1½" x 3½" rectangles. Cut 1 of the strips into 24 squares, 1½" x 1½". Leave the remaining strip uncut.

From the blue stripe:
   Cut 2 strips, 1½" x 42". Cut 1 of the strips into 12 squares, 1½" x 1½". Leave the remaining strip uncut.
   Cut 7 strips, 1" x 42". Cut 2 of the strips into a total of 8 segments, each 5½" wide*, to make 1" x 5½" rectangles for sashing pieces. Leave the remaining sashing strips uncut.

*Your blocks may not measure exactly 5½" wide when sewn. Cut these rectangles a little longer and trim to size after you piece the blocks, if you wish.

From the dark gray print:
   Cut 2 strips, 1½" x 42". Cut the strips into a total of 12 segments, each 5½" wide, to make 1½" x 5½" rectangles.

From the *length* of the black tree print:
   Cut 2 strips, 4½" wide, for side borders.

From the *width* of the remaining black tree print:
   Cut 2 strips, 4½" x 33", for top and bottom borders.

Directions

1. Join the 1½" black star and gray stripe squares to make 12 units as shown; keep the gray stripe running vertically in each unit.

Make 12

2. Join the black star triangles to the trimmed gray stripe rectangles to make 12 units as shown.

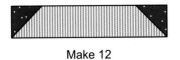

Make 12

3. Join the 1½" blue stripe and gray-and-blue plaid squares to make 12 units as shown. Keep the blue stripe running horizontally in each unit. Join a 1½" x 3½" gray-and-blue plaid rectangle to each of the units as shown.

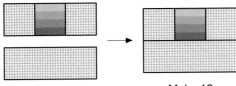

Make 12

4. Join the 1½"-wide gray-and-blue plaid and blue stripe strips to make 1 strip unit as shown. Cut the strip unit into 12 segments, each 2½" wide.

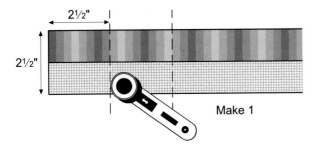

Make 1

5. Piece 12 House blocks as shown.

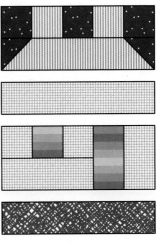

Make 12

6. Set the blocks together with the blue stripe sashing pieces and sashing strips as shown in the quilt photo, cutting the long sashing strips to size as needed. See "Straight Sets" on page 96.
7. Add the black tree-print border as shown in the quilt photo. See "Borders with Straight-Cut Corners" on page 100.
8. Layer with batting and backing; quilt or tie. See page 115 for a quilting suggestion. Bind with straight-grain or bias strips of fabric.

SPLIT NINEPATCH

SPLIT NINEPATCH *by Holly Rebekah Layton, 1995, Anchorage, Alaska, 69" x 70". This Split Ninepatch setting arrangement is commonly associated with quilters of the Perkiomen Valley in Pennsylvania. Holly used a myriad of scraps for her "period piece" and crafted the narrow border from the leftovers.*

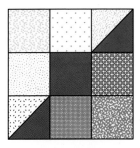

Split Ninepatch
6¾" block

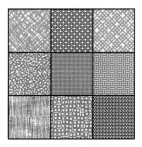

Ninepatch
6¾" block

Dimensions: 72" x 72"

100 blocks (92 Split Ninepatch blocks and 8 Ninepatch blocks), 6¾", set 10 across and 10 down; 2¼"-wide pieced border.

Materials: 44"-wide fabric

1⅓ yds. black print for blocks

1 strip, 2¾" x 42", each of 23 different light prints for blocks and pieced border (Nearest cut is ⅛ yd.)*

1 strip, 6½" x 42", each of 8 more light prints for blocks (You can repeat some of the fabrics used above, if you wish. Nearest cut is ¼ yd.)

1 strip, 2¾" x 42", each of 25 different medium green prints for blocks. (Nearest cut is ⅛ yd.)*

4½ yds. fabric for backing (lengthwise or crosswise seam)

⅝ yd. fabric for ⅜"-wide binding

Batting and thread to finish

Use the same fabric more than once, if you wish.

Cutting:
All measurements include ¼" seams.

From the black print:
   Cut 8 strips, 3⅛" x 42".
   Cut 7 strips, 2¾" x 42".
From *each* of the 6½" x 42" light print strips:
   Cut 1 strip, 3⅛" x 42", for a total of 8 strips.
   Cut 1 strip, 2¾" x 42", for a total of 8 strips.

You now have a total of 31 assorted light strips, 2¾" x 42". From each of any 24 of these strips, cut 3 rectangles, 2¾" x 6", for a total of 72 rectangles for the pieced border. Leave the remaining strips uncut.

From *each* of any 12 medium green print strips:
   Cut 2 squares, 2¾" x 2¾", for a total of 24 loose squares. Leave the remaining strips uncut.

Directions

1. Make ◹: Layer the 3⅛"-wide black and light strips, right sides together, to make 8 contrasting strip pairs. Cut 12 squares, 3⅛" x 3⅛", from each strip pair for a total of 96 layered squares. Cut 92 of the squares once diagonally and chain-piece the resulting triangle pairs to make 184 half-square triangle units.

2. Set aside 7 of the long (2¾" x 42") green strips, all different fabrics. Join the remaining 18 green strips to make 9 all-green strip units as shown. Sew long strips to long strips and short strips to short strips, combining the fabrics at random. Cut the strip units into a total of 116 segments, each 2¾" wide.

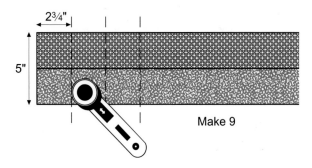

2¾"

5"

Make 9

3. Add a loose 2¾" green square to one end of each of 24 segments cut in step 2. Use as many different fabric combinations as possible. Join these all-green, 3-square segments to make 8 Ninepatch blocks as shown above.

4. Join the long (2¾" x 42") black, light print, and green strips to make 7 strip units as shown. Cut the strip units into a total of 92 segments, each 2¾" wide.

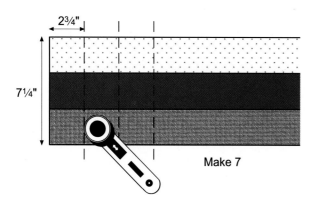

Make 7

5. Join the short (2¾" x 24") light strips to make 12 all-light strip units as shown. Combine the fabrics at random. Cut the strip units into a total of 92 segments, each 2¾" wide.

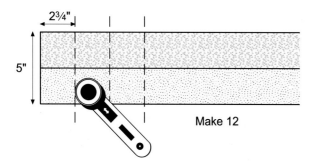

Make 12

6. Using the half-square triangle units made in step 1 and the strip units made in step 5, piece 92 Split Ninepatch blocks as shown.

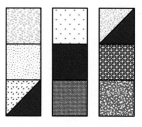

Make 92

7. Set the blocks together in 10 rows of 10 as shown in the quilt photo. *Note that the Ninepatch blocks appear 1 block in from each end of the second and ninth rows, and 4 blocks in from each end of the fourth and seventh rows.* Join the rows.

8. Join the 2¾" x 6" light rectangles to make 4 pieced border strips, each at least 72" long, combining the fabrics at random. Cut some of the rectangles down to 2¾" x 2¾" squares as in the pictured quilt, if you wish. Add the pieced border strips as shown in the quilt photo, trimming the strips as necessary. See "Borders with Straight-Cut Corners" on page 100.

9. Layer with batting and backing; quilt or tie. See page 115 for a quilting suggestion. Bind with straight-grain or bias strips of fabric.

FLYING BIRDS

MIGRATION *by Emily R. McAlister, 1992, Anchorage, Alaska, 44³/₄" x 58¹/₄". Exotic contemporary prints spark up this classic traditional design. The sashing fabric features tiny birds. Emily made this quilt—her fourth—as a way of shaking off "cabin fever," a common winter affliction in these climes. (Collection of Wendy J. Talbott)*

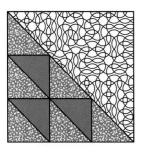

Block A
(red birds)
6" block

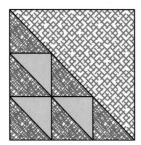

Block B
(blue birds)
6" block

Dimensions: 44¾" x 58¼"

48 blocks (36 Block A, "red birds," and 12 Block B, "blue birds"), 6", set 6 across and 8 down with ¾"-wide sashing; 2½"-wide border.

Materials: 44"-wide fabric

1 piece, 6⅞" x 15", each of 12 different large-scale red, gold, and blue-green prints for large triangles (Nearest cut is ¼ yd.)

1 strip, 2⅞" x 10", each of 18 different red prints or solids for Block A birds (Nearest cut is ⅛ yd.)*

1 strip, 2⅞" x 20", each of 18 different blue-green or gold prints for Block A backgrounds (Nearest cut is ⅛ yd.)*

1 strip, 2⅞" x 10", each of 6 more blue-green prints or solids for Block B birds (Nearest cut is ⅛ yd.)*

1 strip, 2⅞" x 20", each of 6 more red prints for Block B backgrounds (Nearest cut is ⅛ yd.)*

⅝ yd. medium blue print for sashing

⅝ yd. large-scale, multicolored print for seamed border

3 yds. fabric for backing (crosswise seam)

½ yd. fabric for ⅜"-wide binding

Batting and thread to finish

*Use the same fabric more than once, if you wish.

Cutting:

All measurements include ¼" seams.

From each of the 12 large-scale prints:
Cut 2 squares, 6⅞" x 6⅞", for a total of 24 squares. Cut the squares once diagonally to make 48 half-square triangles.

From the medium blue print:
Cut 14 strips, 1¼" x 42". Cut 7 of the strips into a total of 40 rectangles, 1¼" x 6½"*, for sashing pieces. Leave the remaining strips uncut.

*Your blocks may not measure exactly 6½" square when sewn. Cut these rectangles a little longer than 6½" and trim the sashing pieces to size after you piece the blocks, if you wish.

From the large-scale, multicolored print:
Cut 6 strips, 3" x 42", for border.

Directions

1. Start by making 36 red bird blocks (Block A). Sort the 2⅞" x 10" red strips and the 2⅞" x 20" blue-green or gold strips into 18 pleasing sets, each containing 1 red and 1 blue-green or gold strip.

2. Work with 1 set at a time. From one end of the blue-green or gold strip, cut 3 squares, 2⅞" x 2⅞"; cut the squares once diagonally to make 6 loose half-square triangles. Now make ◢ by layering the red strip and the remaining piece of blue-green strip right sides together. From this strip pair, cut 3 squares, 2⅞" x 2⅞". Cut these layered squares once diagonally and chain-piece the resulting triangle pairs to make 6 half-square triangle units.

3. Join the loose half-square triangles and the half-square triangle units you made in step 2 with any 2 of the 6⅞" large-scale print triangles to make 2 Block A as shown. Repeat steps 2 and 3 with the remaining sets to make a total of 36 Block A.

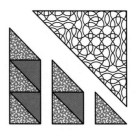

Make 36

4. Now make the blue bird blocks (Block B). Sort the 2⅞" x 10" blue-green strips and the 2⅞" x 20" red strips into 6 pleasing sets, each containing 1 red and 1 blue-green strip.

5. Work with 1 set at a time. From one end of the red strip, cut 3 squares, 2⅞" x 2⅞"; cut the squares once diagonally to make 6 loose half-square triangles. Now make ◺ by layering the blue-green strip and the remaining piece of red strip, right sides together. From this strip pair, cut 3 squares, 2⅞" x 2⅞". Cut these layered squares once diagonally and chain-piece the resulting triangle pairs to make 6 half-square triangle units.

6. Join the loose half-square triangles and the half-square triangle units you made in step 5 with any 2 of the 6⅞" large-scale print triangles to make 2 Block B as shown on page 68. Repeat steps 5 and 6 with the remaining sets to make a total of 12 Block B.

7. Set the blocks together with the medium blue sashing pieces and strips as shown in the quilt photo, cutting the long sashing strips to size as needed. See "Straight Sets" on page 96.

8. Add the multicolored print border, seaming strips as necessary. See "Borders with Straight-Cut Corners" on page 100.

9. Layer with batting and backing; quilt or tie. See page 115 for a quilting suggestion. Bind with straight-grain or bias strips of fabric.

DOUBLE SQUARES

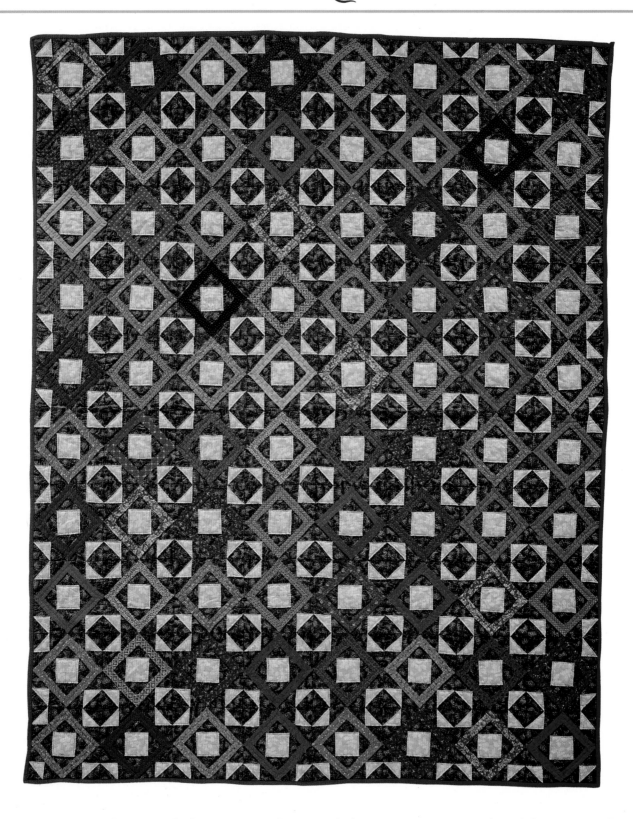

JACK IN THE BOX *by Doris Rhodes, 1992, Anchorage, Alaska, 72" x 90". Doris adapted this pattern, also known as "Jack in the Pulpit," from a 100-year-old quilt in her collection. The eclectic array of red prints in many different values is balanced by the repetitive use of blue and beige background fabrics.*

Dimensions:
72" x 90"

80 blocks, 9", set 8 across and 10 down; finished without a border.

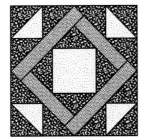

Double Squares
9" block

Materials: *44"-wide fabric*

4½ yds. blue print for blocks
2⅛ yds. beige print for blocks
⅛ yd. each of 27 different red prints for blocks*
5½ yds. fabric for backing (lengthwise seam)
¾ yd. fabric for ⅜"-wide binding
Batting and thread to finish

Note that the red prints in this quilt include clear reds, maroons, roses, corals, and red-violets in values ranging from medium to dark. Use the same fabric more than once, if you wish.

Cutting:
All measurements include ¼" seams.

From the blue print:
Cut 9 strips, 4⅜" x 42". Cut the strips into a total of 80 squares, 4⅜" x 4⅜". Cut the squares twice diagonally to make 320 quarter-square triangles.
Cut 38 strips, 3⅛" x 42". Cut 25 of the strips into a total of 320 squares, 3⅛" x 3⅛". Cut the squares once diagonally to make 640 half-square triangles. Leave the remaining 13 strips uncut.

From the beige print:
Cut 8 strips, 3⅝" x 42". Cut the strips into a total of 80 squares, 3⅝" x 3⅝".
Cut 13 strips, 3⅛" x 42".

From *each* of the assorted red prints:
Cut 2 strips, 1½" x 42", for a total of 54 strips. From each strip, cut 3 rectangles, 1½" x 4⅞", and 3 rectangles, 1½" x 6⅞", for a total of 162 short rectangles and 162 long rectangles. Two of the short rectangles and 2 of the long rectangles will be extras.

Directions

1. Make : Layer the 3⅛"-wide blue and beige strips, right sides together, to make 13 contrasting strip pairs. Cut 13 squares, 3⅛" x 3⅛", from each strip pair for a total of 169 layered squares. Cut the squares once diagonally and chain-piece the resulting triangle pairs to make 338 half-square triangle units. You will have 18 extras.

2. Join the 3⅝" beige squares and the 4⅜" blue quarter-square triangles to make 80 units as shown.

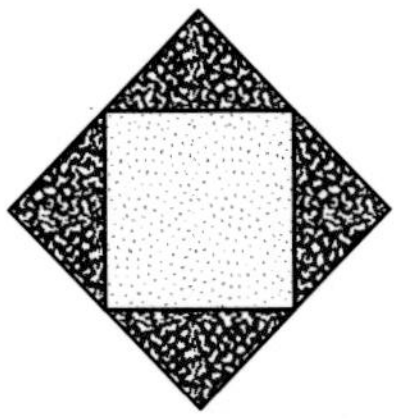

Make 80

3. Join the blue/beige half-square triangle units and the 3⅛" blue triangles to make 320 units as shown.

Make 320

4. Piece 80 Double Squares blocks as shown. Use rectangles cut from just 1 red print in each of the blocks.

Make 80

5. Set the blocks together in 10 rows of 8 as shown in the quilt photo; join the rows.

6. Layer with batting and backing; quilt or tie. See page 116 for a quilting suggestion. Bind with straight-grain or bias strips of fabric.

71

LOUISIANA

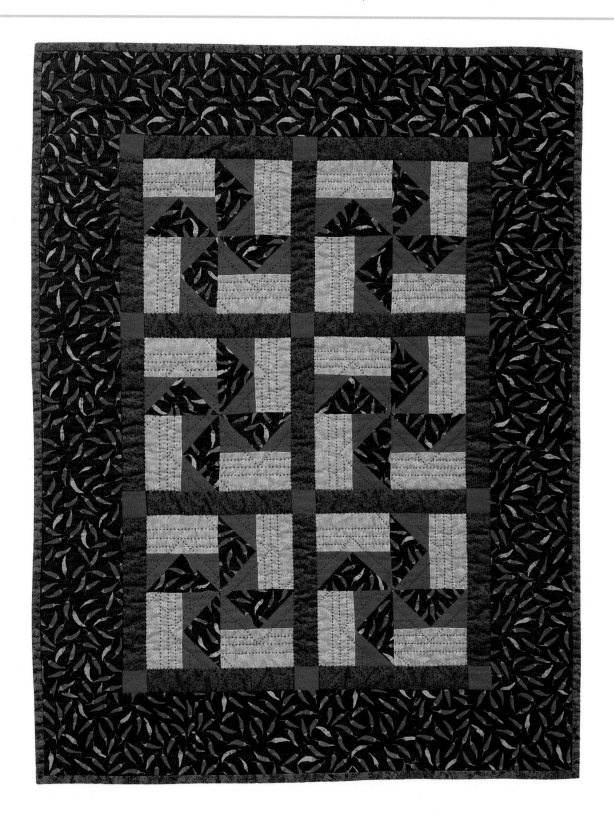

TABASCO by Judy Dafoe Hopkins, 1994, Anchorage, Alaska, 28³/₄" x 38".
Judy used Tabasco®-bottle colors and a chili pepper print for this fiery little quilt. The block choice is particularly appropriate—the famous pepper sauce is made in Avery Island, Louisiana. Quilted with perle cotton.

Louisiana
8" block

Dimensions: 28¾" x 38

6 blocks, 8", set 2 across and 3 down with 1¼"-wide sashing and sashing squares; 4½"-wide border.

Materials: 44"-wide fabric

⅓ yd. red print for blocks and sashing squares
⅓ yd. tan print for blocks
⅞ yd. chili pepper print for blocks and border
⅓ yd. green print for sashing
1⅓ yds. fabric for backing
⅜ yd. fabric for ⅜"-wide binding
Batting and thread to finish

Cutting:
All measurements include ¼" seams.

From the red print:
Cut 2 strips, 2⅞" x 42". Cut the strips into a total of 24 squares, 2⅞" x 2⅞". Cut the squares once diagonally to make 48 half-square triangles.
Cut 1 strip, 1¾" x 42". Cut the strip into 12 squares, 1¾" x 1¾", for sashing squares.

From the tan print:
Cut 3 strips, 2½" x 42". Cut the strips into a total of 24 segments, each 4½" wide, to make 2½" x 4½" rectangles.

From the chili pepper print:
Cut 1 strip, 5¼" x 42". Cut the strip into 6 squares, 5¼" x 5¼". Cut the squares twice diagonally to make 24 quarter-square triangles.
Cut 4 strips, 5" x 42", for border.

From the green print:
Cut 1 strip, 8½"* x 42". Cut the strip into 17 segments, each 1¾" wide, to make sashing pieces 1¾" x 8½".

* Your blocks may not measure exactly 8½" square when sewn. Cut this strip a little wider than 8½" and trim the sashing pieces to size after you piece the blocks, if you wish.

Directions

1. Join the 2⅞" red half-square triangles and the 5¼" chili pepper print quarter-square triangles to make 24 units as shown.

Make 24

2. Piece 6 Louisiana blocks as shown.

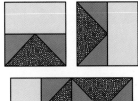

Make 6

3. Set the blocks together in 3 rows of 2 with the green sashing pieces and red sashing squares as shown in the quilt photo; join the rows. See "Straight Sets" on page 96.

4. Add the chili pepper print border as shown in the quilt photo. See "Borders with Straight-Cut Corners" on page 100.

5. Layer with batting and backing; quilt or tie. See page 116 for a quilting suggestion. Bind with straight-grain or bias strips of fabric.

GENTLEMAN'S FANCY

GENTLEMAN'S FANCY *by Mary Jo Wenrick, 1995, Girdwood, Alaska, 60" x 72½".*
This is one of the many traditional designs that form stars when the blocks are set together. Mary Jo's use of
prints in a variety of visual textures is very effective. The quilt was crow-footed with perle cotton.

Dimensions:
60" x 72"

20 blocks, 12", set 4 across and 5 down; 6"-wide border.

Gentleman's Fancy
12" block

Materials:
44"-wide fabric

⅞ yd. beige print for block backgrounds

⅞ yd. multicolored floral print for blocks

½ yd. each of 2 different red-violet prints for block corners

2½ yds. dark green print for blocks and border

3¾ yds. fabric for backing (crosswise seam)

⅝ yd. fabric for ⅜"-wide binding

Batting and thread to finish

Cutting:
All measurements include ¼" seams.

From the beige print:
Cut 5 strips, 5¼" x 42". Cut the strips into a total of 40 squares, 5¼" x 5¼". Cut the squares twice diagonally to make 160 quarter-square triangles.

From the multicolored floral print:
Cut 5 strips, 4⅞" x 42". Cut the strips into a total of 40 squares, 4⅞" x 4⅞". Cut the squares once diagonally to make 80 half-square triangles.

From *each* of the 2 red-violet prints:
Cut 3 strips, 4⅞" x 42", for a total of 6 strips. Cut the strips into a total of 40 squares, 4⅞" x 4⅞" (20 from each fabric). Cut the squares once diagonally to make 80 half-square triangles.

From the dark green print:
Cut 3 strips, 4½" x 42". Cut the strips into a total of 20 squares, 4½" x 4½".

From the *length* of the remaining dark green print, cut 4 strips, 6½" wide, for border.

From the remaining piece of dark green print, cut 14 strips, 5¼" x 16". Cut the strips into a total of 40 squares, 5¼" x 5¼". Cut the squares twice diagonally to make 160 quarter-square triangles.

Directions

1. Using 80 of the 5¼" beige quarter-square triangles and the 4½" dark green squares, make 20 units.

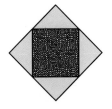

Make 20

2. Using the 5¼" dark green quarter-square triangles and the 4⅞" floral half-square triangles, make 80 units.

Make 80

3. Join 40 of the units made in step 2 to the units made in step 1 to make 20 units.

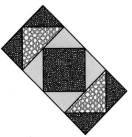

Make 20

4. Join 80 beige quarter-square triangles to the remaining units you made in step 2 to make 40 units.

Make 40

5. Piece 20 Gentleman's Fancy blocks as shown.

Make 20

6. Set the blocks together in 5 rows of 4 as shown in the quilt photo; join the rows.

7. Add the dark green border. See "Borders with Straight-Cut Corners" on page 100.

8. Layer with batting and backing; quilt or tie. See page 116 for a quilting suggestion. Bind with straight-grain or bias strips of fabric.

BROKEN WHEEL

BROKEN WHEEL *by Trish DeLong, 1995, Fairbanks, Alaska, 64¹/₂" x 85".*
This design is also known as "Rolling Stone" and "Wedding Ring." The dramatic Oriental print
and the interesting background fabric combine to make a truly elegant quilt. Quilted by Janet Myers.

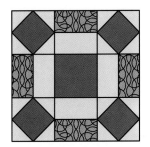

Broken Wheel
12¾" block

Dimensions: 69¼" x 86¼"

12 blocks, 12¾", set 3 across and 4 down with
4¼"-wide sashing and pieced sashing squares;
1"-wide inner border, 6"-wide outer border.

Materials: 44"-wide fabric

3 yds. light gold print for blocks and sashing
1⅛ yds. blue print for blocks and seamed inner border
2¼ yds. red print for blocks and seamed outer border
5¼ yds. fabric for backing (lengthwise seam)
¾ yd. fabric for ⅜"-wide binding
Batting and thread to finish

Cutting:
All measurements include ¼" seams.

From the light gold print:
   Cut 8 strips, 3" x 42". Cut the strips into a
      total of 108 squares, 3" x 3". Cut the
      squares once diagonally to make 216 half-
      square triangles.
   Cut 7 strips, 2⅝" x 42".
   Cut 13 strips, 4¾" x 42". Cut 6 of the strips
      into a total of 17 rectangles, 4¾" x
      13¼"*, for sashing pieces. Leave the
      remaining 7 strips uncut.

*Your blocks may not measure exactly 13¼" square when sewn.
Cut these rectangles a little longer and trim the sashing pieces to
size after you piece the blocks, if you wish.

From the blue print:
   Cut 4 strips, 3½" x 42". Cut the strips into a
      total of 48 squares, 3½" x 3½".
   Cut 2 strips, 4¾" x 42".
   Cut 7 strips, 1½" x 42", for inner border.

From the red print:
   Cut 1 strip, 3½" x 42". Cut the strip into 6
      squares, 3½" x 3½".
   Cut 7 strips, 2⅝" x 42".
   Cut 8 strips, 6½" x 42", for outer border.

Directions

1. Join the light gold triangles and the blue and
   red squares to make 48 gold and blue units (for
   blocks) and 6 gold and red units (for pieced
   sashing squares) as shown.

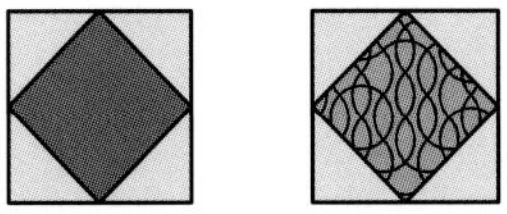

   Make 48   Make 6

2. Join 3 each of the 2⅝"-wide light gold and red
   strips to make 3 strip units as shown. Cut the
   strip units into a total of 24 segments, each
   4¾" wide.

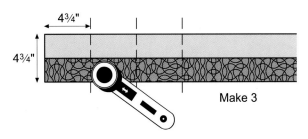

   Make 3

3. Join the remaining 2⅝"-wide light gold and red
   strips and the 4¾"-wide blue strips to make 2
   strip units as shown. Cut the strip units into a
   total of 12 segments, each 4¾" wide.

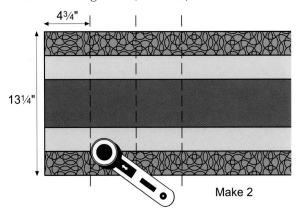

   Make 2

4. Piece 12 Broken Wheel blocks as shown.

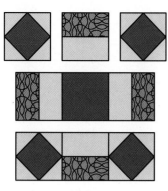

Make 12

5. Set the blocks together with the light gold sashing pieces and the pieced sashing squares as shown in the quilt photo. Seam the remaining 4¾"-wide light gold strips as necessary and add to the outside edges of the quilt.

6. Add the blue inner border and red outer border as shown in the quilt photo, seaming strips as necessary. See "Borders with Straight-Cut Corners" on page 100.

7. Layer with batting and backing; quilt or tie. See page 116 for a quilting suggestion. Bind with straight-grain or bias strips of fabric.

SUMMER WINDS

CARRIED AWAY *by Judy Dafoe Hopkins, 1994, Anchorage, Alaska, 82$\frac{1}{4}$" x 103$\frac{3}{4}$".*
There's nothing like a good stripe to add some life to a collection of scrappy blocks. Can you spot the block with the mismatched patch? Quilted by the Willing Workers Quilting Club.

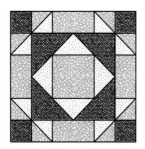

Summer Winds
10½" block

Dimensions: 83½" x 104½"

35 blocks (18 Summer Winds and 17 alternate blocks), 10½", set 5 across and 7 down; 7"-wide inner border, 8½"-wide outer border.

Materials: 44"-wide fabric

1 strip, 4" x 25", each of 18 different orange and rust prints for blocks (Nearest cut is ⅛ yd.)

1 strip, 4¾" x 17", each of 18 different light blue prints for blocks (Nearest cut is ¼ yd.)

1 strip, 4⅜" x 20", each of 18 different medium and dark blue prints for blocks (Nearest cut is ¼ yd.)

3½ yds. dark blue stripe for alternate blocks and inner border

2⅝ yds. tone-on-tone navy blue print for outer border

7⅝ yds. fabric for backing (2 crosswise seams), or use 3⅛ yds. of 90"-wide backing fabric

¾ yd. fabric for ⅜"-wide binding

Batting and thread to finish

Cutting:
All measurements include ¼" seams.

From *each* of the 18 orange and rust strips:
Cut 1 square, 4" x 4", and 4 rectangles, 2¼" x 4", for a total of 18 squares and 72 rectangles.
From each of the remaining pieces, cut 1 strip, 2⅝" x 12", for a total of 18 strips.

From *each* of the 18 light blue strips:
Cut 1 square, 4¾" x 4¾", for a total of 18 squares. Cut the squares twice diagonally to make 72 quarter-square triangles.
From each of the remaining pieces, cut 1 strip, 2⅝" x 12", for a total of 18 strips.

From *each* of the 18 medium and dark blue strips:
Cut 2 squares, 4⅜" x 4⅜", for a total of 36 squares. Cut the squares once diagonally to make 72 half-square triangles.
Cut 4 squares, 2¼" x 2¼", for a total of 72 squares.

From the dark blue stripe:
Cut 3 strips, 7½" x 42", for seamed inner border (top and bottom)
From the *length* of the remaining piece of dark blue stripe, cut 2 strips, 7½" x 90", for inner border (sides)
From the remaining piece of dark blue stripe, cut 17 squares, 11" x 11", for alternate blocks.

From the *length* of the tone-on-tone navy blue print:
Cut 4 strips, 9" wide, for outer border.

Directions

1. Make ◢: Layer the 2⅝"-wide orange and rust strips and the 2⅝"-wide light blue strips, right sides together, to make 18 contrasting strip pairs. Cut 4 squares, 2⅝" x 2⅝", from each strip pair for a total of 72 layered squares. Cut the squares once diagonally and chain-piece the resulting triangle pairs to make 144 half-square triangle units.

2. Using the same fabric combinations you used in step 1, join the 4¾" light blue quarter-square triangles to the 4" orange and rust squares to make 18 units as shown.

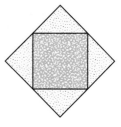

Make 18

3. Join the 4⅜" medium or dark blue half-square triangles to the units you made in step 2 to make 18 units as shown.

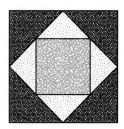

Make 18

4. Piece 18 Summer Winds blocks as shown. Use just 1 orange, 1 light blue, and 1 medium or dark blue fabric in each block.

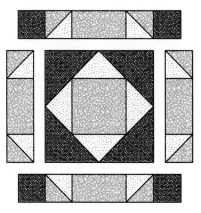

Make 18

5. Set the blocks together with the dark blue striped alternate blocks as shown in the quilt photo; join the rows.

6. Add the dark blue striped inner border as shown in the quilt photo. Add the top and bottom borders first, seaming the 7½" x 42" blue striped strips as necessary, then add the side borders. See "Borders with Straight-Cut Corners" on page 100.

7. Add the navy blue outer border as shown in the quilt photo. Join the side pieces first, then the top and bottom.

8. Layer with batting and backing; quilt or tie. See page 117 for a quilting suggestion. Bind with straight-grain or bias strips of fabric.

FOUR-FOUR TIME

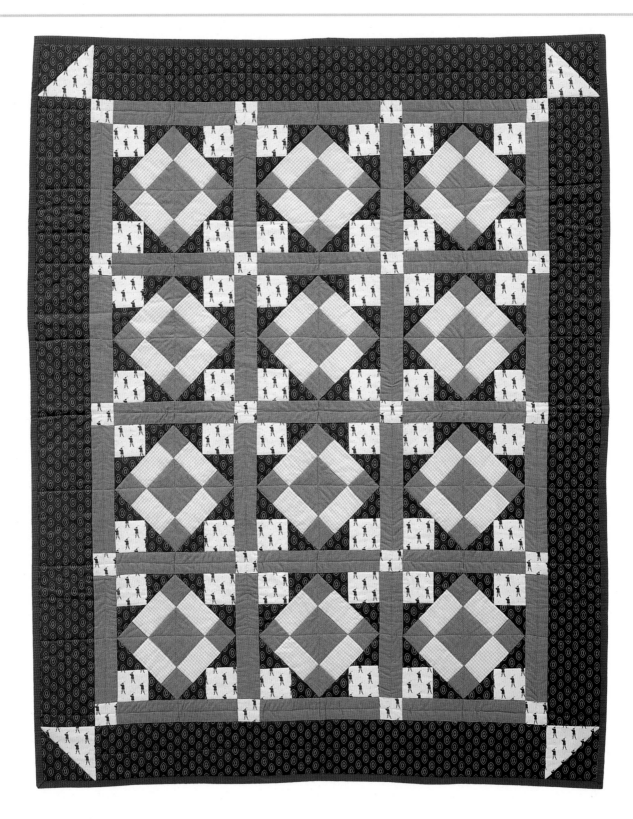

THE BOSS CAN GOLF *by Kay Dennis, 1994, Anchorage, Alaska, 54" x 67".*
The traditional Four-Four Time block might more appropriately be called "Fore-Fore Time" in this incarnation,
which sports a charming golfer pictorial print. Made in a Debbie Caffrey class. (Collection of Terry Cerney)

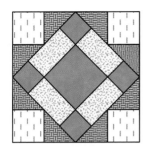

Four-Four Time
12" block

Dimensions: 54" x 68"

12 blocks, 12", set 3 across and 4 down with 2"-wide sashing and sashing squares; 5"-wide border with pieced corner squares.

Materials: 44"-wide fabric

⅞ yd. golfer pictorial or other light print for blocks, sashing squares, and pieced border corners
⅔ yd. light plaid for blocks
1⅜ yds. butterscotch check for blocks and sashing
1¾ yds. dark green print for blocks and border
3½ yds. fabric for backing (crosswise seam)
⅝ yd. fabric for ⅜"-wide binding
Batting and thread to finish

Cutting:
All measurements include ¼" seams.

From the golfer print:
Cut 4 strips, 3½" x 42". Cut the strips into a total of 48 squares, 3½" x 3½".
Cut 2 strips, 2½" x 42". Cut the strips into a total of 20 squares, 2½" x 2½", for sashing squares.
Cut 2 squares, 5⅞" x 5⅞". Cut the squares once diagonally to make 4 half-square triangles for pieced border corners.
From the light plaid:
Cut 2 strips, 4¾" x 42".
Cut 4 strips, 2⅝" x 42".
From the butterscotch check:
Cut 2 strips, 4¾" x 42".
Cut 4 strips, 2⅝" x 42".

Cut 2 strips, 12½"* x 42". Cut the strips into a total of 31 segments, each 2½" wide, to make 2½" x 12½" rectangles for sashing pieces.

Your blocks may not measure exactly 12½" square when sewn. Cut this strip a little wider and trim the sashing pieces to size after you piece the blocks, if you wish.

From the *length* of the dark green print:
Cut 4 strips, 5½" wide, for border.
From the remaining piece of dark green print:
Cut 10 strips, 3⅞" x 20". Cut the strips into a total of 48 squares, 3⅞" x 3⅞". Cut the squares once diagonally to make 96 half-square triangles.
Cut 2 squares, 5⅞" x 5⅞". Cut the squares once diagonally to make 4 half-square triangles for pieced border corners.

Directions

1. Join the 2⅝"-wide butterscotch strips and the 4¾"-wide light plaid strips to make 2 strip units as shown. Cut the strip units into a total of 24 segments, each 2⅝" wide.

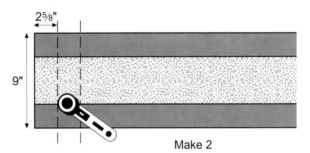

Make 2

2. Join the 2⅝"-wide light plaid strips and the 4¾"-wide butterscotch strips to make 2 strip units as shown. Cut the strip units into a total of 12 segments, each 4¾" wide.

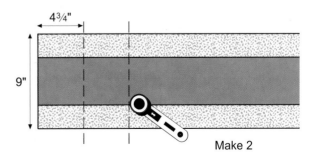

Make 2

3. Join the segments you cut in steps 1 and 2 to make 12 units as shown.

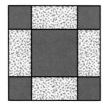

Make 12

4. Join the units you made in step 3 with the 3½" golfer print squares and the 3⅞" dark green triangles to make 12 Four-Four Time blocks as shown.

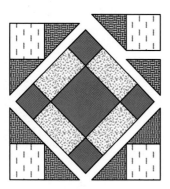

Make 12

5. Join the 5⅞" golfer print and dark green triangles to make 4 half-square triangle units for the pieced border corners as shown.

Make 4

6. Set the blocks together with the butterscotch sashing pieces and golfer print sashing squares as shown in the quilt photo. See "Straight Sets" on page 96.
7. Add the dark green border with half-square triangle corner squares. See "Borders with Corner Squares" on page 101.
8. Layer with batting and backing; quilt or tie. See page 117 for a quilting suggestion. Bind with straight-grain or bias strips of fabric.

A Brighter Day

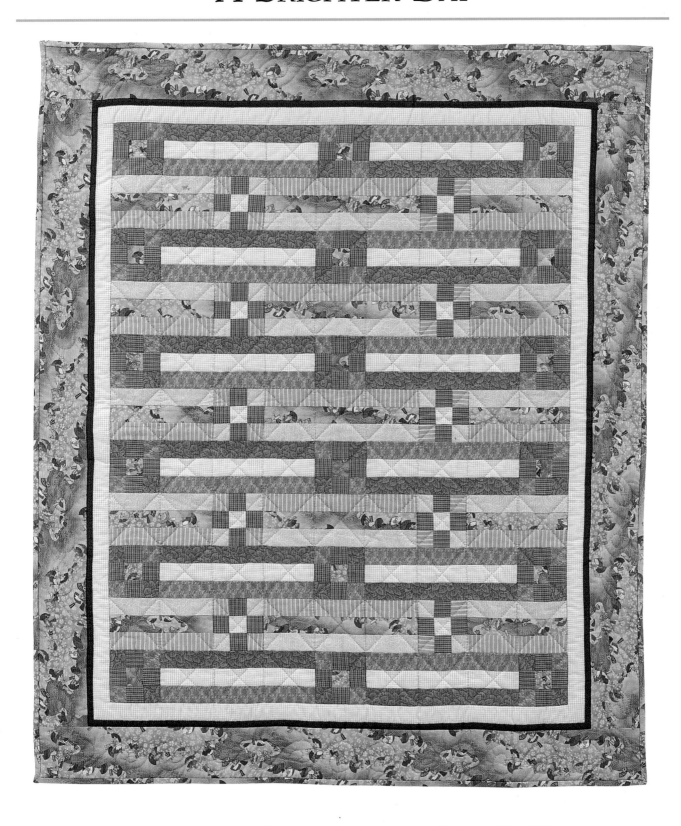

Fantasia by Anne Richardson, 1994, Anchorage, Alaska, $42^3/4''$ x $50''$.
Sophisticated fabric and color choices make this simple quilt very special.
The narrow purple border is an important addition. Quilted by the Indiana Amish.

This pattern was inspired by a Katherine Courtney quilt, originally published in *Old Fashioned Patchwork* magazine (Summer 1993, page 35); the design is used with Katherine's permission.

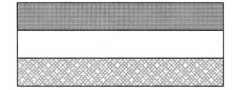

Ninepatch
3¾" block

Strip unit

Dimensions: 44¾" x 52¼"

28 Ninepatch blocks, 3³/₄", 17 strip units, 3³/₄" x 11¹/₄", and 10 strip units, 3³/₄" x 7¹/₂", set together in 11 rows; 1¹/₄"-wide inner border, ¹/₂"-wide middle border, 3³/₄"-wide outer border.

Materials: 44"-wide fabric

¹/₂ yd. light taupe print for blocks and seamed inner border (Fabric 1)

¹/₃ yd. each of 2 more light taupe prints for blocks (Fabrics 2 and 3)

¹/₂ yd. medium taupe print for blocks (Fabric 4)

1¹/₈ yds. large-scale coral print for blocks and seamed outer border (Fabric 5)

³/₈ yd. each of 2 more medium coral prints for blocks (Fabrics 6 and 7)

¹/₄ yd. purple print for seamed middle border

3 yds. fabric for backing (crosswise seam)

¹/₂ yd. fabric for ³/₈"-wide binding

Batting and thread to finish

Note: *Paste a snip of each of Fabrics 1–7 to a card and number the snips. Use this for reference during the cutting and assembly process.*

Cutting:
All measurements include ¼" seams.

From Fabric 1:
    Cut 9 strips, 1³/₄" x 42", for blocks and inner border.
From each of Fabrics 2 and 3:
    Cut 5 strips, 1³/₄" x 42", for a total of 10 strips.

From Fabric 4:
    Cut 7 strips, 1³/₄" x 42", for blocks.
From Fabric 5:
    Cut 6 strips, 4¹/₄" x 42", for outer border.
    Cut 5 strips, 1³/₄" x 42", for blocks.
From each of Fabrics 6 and 7:
    Cut 6 strips, 1³/₄" x 42", for a total of 12 strips.
From the purple print:
    Cut 5 strips, 1" x 42", for middle border.

Directions

1. Join strips cut from Fabrics 7, 1, and 6 to make 4 strip units as shown. Cut the strip units into a total of 12 segments, each 11³/₄" wide.

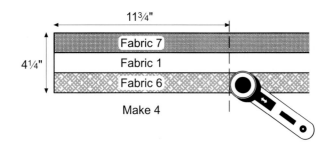

Make 4

2. Join strips cut from Fabrics 2, 5, and 3 to make 4 strip units as shown. Cut 2 of the strip units into a total of 5 segments, each 11³/₄" wide. Cut the remaining 2 strip units into a total of 10 segments, each 8" wide.

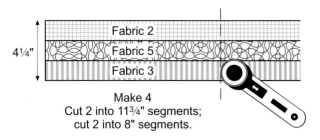

Make 4
Cut 2 into 11³/₄" segments; cut 2 into 8" segments.

3. Join strips cut from Fabrics 7, 4, and 6 to make 2 strip units as shown. Cut the strip units into a total of 36 segments, each 1³/₄" wide.

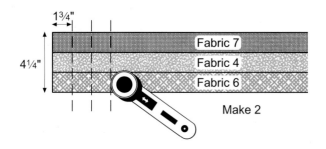

Make 2

4. Join strips cut from Fabrics 4 and 5 to make 1 strip unit as shown. Cut the strip unit into 18 segments, each 1¾" wide.

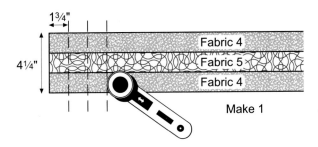

Make 1

5. Join the segments you cut in steps 3 and 4 to make 18 Ninepatch blocks as shown.

Make 18

6. Join strips cut from Fabrics 2, 4, and 3 to make 1 strip unit as shown. Cut the strip unit into 20 segments, each 1¾" wide.

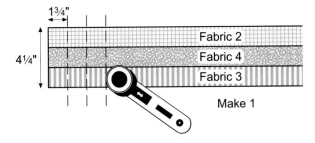

Make 1

7. Join strips cut from Fabrics 4 and 1 to make 1 strip unit as shown. Cut the strip unit into 10 segments, each 1¾" wide.

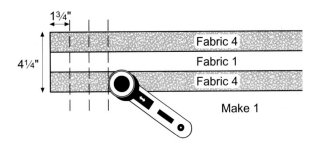

Make 1

8. Join the segments you cut in steps 6 and 7 to make 10 Ninepatch blocks as shown.

Make 10

9. Join the segments cut in steps 1 and 2 and blocks assembled in steps 5 and 8 to make 11 rows as shown in the quilt photo. Watch how you orient the Ninepatch blocks and the strip-unit segments. Join the rows.

10. Add Fabric 1 inner border, purple print middle border, and Fabric 5 outer border as shown in the quilt photo, seaming strips as necessary. See "Borders with Straight-Cut Corners" on page 100.

11. Layer with batting and backing; quilt or tie. See page 117 for a quilting suggestion. Bind with straight-grain or bias strips of fabric.

Oregon Trail

CHINA BLUE by Kathleen Urban Bungart, 1991, Fairbanks, Alaska, 76" x 76". Kathleen crafted this original Judy Martin design in soothing blues. Several of the blocks were made by friends; Kathleen provided the focus fabrics, and The 13 Easy Piecers completed the blocks with prints from their personal collections.

(handwritten:) Lord's Acre 2002
36 × 36 Blocks
Quilted By

Dimensions:
80" x 80"

25 blocks, 12", set on point with side setting triangles; 6"-wide border

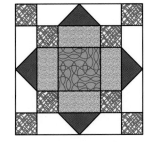

Oregon Trail
12" block

Note: *The Oregon Trail block pattern, an original design by Judy Martin, first appeared in* Judy Martin's Ultimate Book of Quilt Block Patterns©,*1988. Used by permission.*

Materials: 44"-wide fabric

½ yd. large-scale blue floral print for block centers
1 yd. medium-scale blue floral print for block corners
1 strip, 2½" x 42", each of 25 different light prints for block backgrounds (Nearest cut is ⅛ yd.)*
1 strip, 5¼" x 28", each of 5 different dark blue solids or tone-on-tone prints for blocks (Nearest cut is ¼ yd.)
1 strip, 2½" x 19", each of 25 different medium blue prints for blocks (Nearest cut is ⅛ yd.)*
1⅛ yds. white-on-white print for setting triangles
1⅝ yds. dark blue print for seamed border
7¼ yds. fabric for backing (2 crosswise seams), or use 2½ yds. of 90"-wide backing fabric
¾ yd. fabric for ⅜"-wide binding
Batting and thread to finish

**Use the same fabric more than once, if you wish.*

Cutting:
All measurements include ¼" seams.

From the large-scale blue floral print:
Cut 3 strips, 4½" x 42". Cut the strips into a total of 25 squares, 4½" x 4½". *(handwritten: 36)*

From the medium-scale blue floral print:
Cut 13 strips, 2½" x 42". Cut the strips into a total of 200 squares, 2½" x 2½". *(handwritten: 288)*

From the 25 light strips:
Work with 1 fabric at a time. From the first fabric, cut 8 rectangles, 2½" x 4⅞". Trim the corners at a 45° angle to make 4 A and 4 B trimmed rectangles as shown. Repeat with the remaining light strips for *(handwritten: 288, 288)*

a total of 200 trimmed rectangles, 100 A and 100 B.

Trim the corners at a 45° angle.

From *each* of the 5 dark blue solids or tone-on-tone prints:
Cut 5 squares, 5¼" x 5¼", for a total of 25 squares. Cut the squares twice diagonally to make 100 quarter-square triangles. *(handwritten: 144)*

From *each* of the 25 medium blue strips:
Cut 4 rectangles, 2½" x 4½", for a total of 100 rectangles. *(handwritten: 144)*

From the white-on-white print:
Cut 3 squares, 18¼" x 18¼". Cut the squares twice diagonally to make 12 quarter-square triangles for side setting triangles. *(handwritten: 4, 16)*
Cut 2 squares, 9⅜" x 9⅜". Cut the squares once diagonally to make 4 half-square triangles for corner setting triangles.

From the dark blue print:
Cut 8 strips, 6½" x 42", for border.

Directions

1. Piece 25 Oregon Trail blocks as shown. In each block, use just 1 fabric for the medium blue rectangles, 1 fabric for the dark blue quarter-square triangles, and 1 fabric for the light trimmed rectangles.

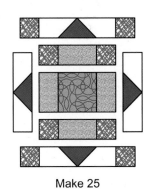

Make 25

2. Set the blocks and setting pieces together in diagonal rows as shown in the quilt photo; join the rows. See "Assembling On-Point Quilts" on page 98.

3. Add the dark blue print border as shown in the quilt photo, seaming strips as necessary. See "Borders with Straight-Cut Corners" on page 100.

4. Layer with batting and backing; quilt or tie. See page 117 for a quilting suggestion. Bind with straight-grain or bias strips of fabric.

LADY OF THE LAKE

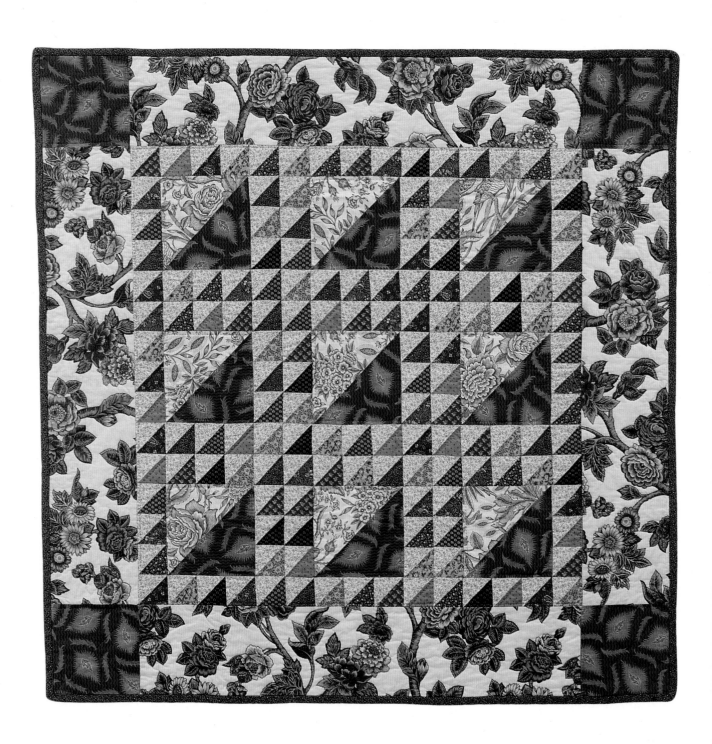

NIMUE *by Dee Morrow, 1995, Anchorage, Alaska, 41½" x 41½".*
Dee has done up the popular Lady of the Lake design in antique-reproduction prints.
This small but special nine-block quilt is a great place to try out any of those exciting new fabric lines.

Lady of the Lake
10" block

Dimensions: 42" x 42"

9 blocks, 10", set 3 across and 3 down; 6"-wide border with corner squares.

Materials: 44"-wide fabric

½ yd. purple print for large triangles and corner squares

¼ yd. large-scale light green floral print for large triangles

¾ yd. light green print for small triangles

1 strip, 2⅞" x 25", each of 9 different medium-to-dark purple and green prints for small triangles (Nearest cut is ⅛ yd.)

⅞ yd. large-scale multicolored floral print for border

2¾ yds. fabric for backing (lengthwise or crosswise seam)

½ yd. fabric for ⅜"-wide binding

Batting and thread to finish

Cutting:
All measurements include ¼" seams.

From the purple print:
Cut 1 strip, 6⅞" x 42.
Cut 1 strip, 6½" x 42". Cut the strip into 4 squares, 6½" x 6½", for border corners.

From the large-scale light green floral print:
Cut 1 strip, 6⅞" x 42".

From the *length* of the light green print:
Cut 9 strips, 2⅞" x 25".

From the multicolored floral print:
Cut 4 strips, 6½" x 42", for border.

Directions

1. Make ◳: Layer the 6⅞"-wide purple and large-scale light green floral strips, right sides together, to make 1 contrasting strip pair. Cut 5 layered squares, 6⅞" x 6⅞", from the strip pair. Cut the squares once diagonally and chain-piece the resulting triangle pairs to make 10 half-square triangle units. One unit is extra.

2. Make ◥: Layer the nine 2⅞"-wide light green and the 9 medium/dark purple and green strips, right sides together, to make 9 contrasting strip pairs. Cut 8 squares, 2⅞" x 2⅞", from each strip pair for a total of 72 layered squares. Cut the squares once diagonally and chain-piece the resulting triangle pairs to make 144 half-square triangle units.

3. Piece 9 Lady of the Lake blocks as shown.

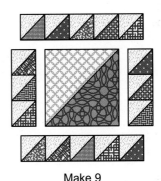

Make 9

4. Set the blocks together in 3 rows of 3 as shown in the quilt photo; join the rows.

5. Add the multicolored floral border and purple corner squares as shown in the quilt photo. See "Borders with Corner Squares" on page 101.

6. Layer with batting and backing; quilt or tie. See page 118 for a quilting suggestion. Bind with straight-grain or bias strips of fabric.

PINWHEEL MOSAIC

SPIN DOCTOR *by Judy Dafoe Hopkins, 1994, Anchorage, Alaska, 61" x 73". Judy converted the traditional Mosaic 9 pattern to a bar format, which reduced the number of seams. The windowpane-check border quietly reflects the colors of the quilt. Quilted by Peggy Hinchey. (Collection of Robert Pittman)*

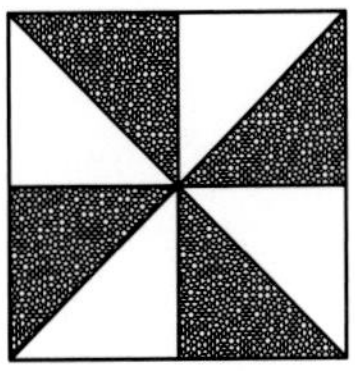

Block A
6" block

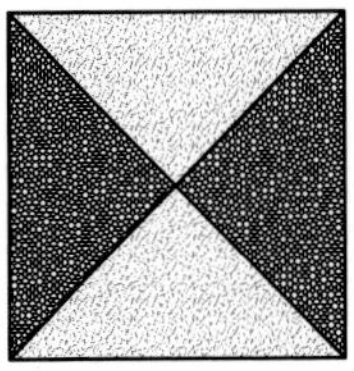

Block B
6" block

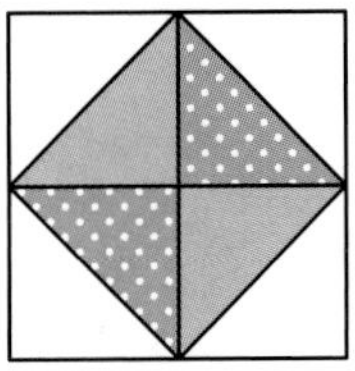

Block C
6" block

Dimensions: 61½" x 73½"

63 blocks (20 Block A, 31 Block B, and 12 Block C), 6", set 7 across and 9 down with half blocks and quarter blocks; ¾"-wide inner border, 6"-wide outer border.

Materials: 44"-wide fabric

1⅝ yds. brown print for blocks
1 yd. ivory print for blocks
1⅛ yds. beige leaf print for blocks
⅓ yd. red print for blocks
⅓ yd. tan print for blocks
⅓ yd. dark red print for seamed inner border
1⅞ yds. tan plaid for outer border
3⅞ yds. fabric for backing (crosswise seam)
⅝ yd. fabric for ⅜"-wide binding
Batting and thread to finish

Cutting:
All measurements include ¼" seams.

From the brown print:
Cut 4 strips, 3⅞" x 42".
Cut 5 strips, 7¼" x 42". Cut 1 of the strips into 5 squares, 7¼" x 7¼". Cut the squares twice diagonally to make 20 quarter-square triangles. Two of these triangles will be extras. Leave the remaining strips uncut.

From the ivory print:
Cut 8 strips, 3⅞" x 42".

From the beige leaf print:
Cut 2 strips, 3⅞" x 42". Cut the strips into a total of 18 squares, 3⅞" x 3⅞". Cut the squares once diagonally to make 36 half-square triangles.
Cut 4 strips, 7¼" x 42".

From the red print:
Cut 2 strips, 3⅞" x 42".

From the tan print:
Cut 2 strips, 3⅞" x 42".

From the dark red print:
Cut 6 strips, 1¼" x 42", for inner border.

From the *length* of the tan plaid:
Cut 4 strips, 6½" wide, for outer border.

Directions

1. Make : Layer the 3⅞"-wide brown strips and 4 of the 3⅞"-wide ivory strips, right sides together, to make 4 contrasting strip pairs. Cut 10 squares, 3⅞" x 3⅞", from each strip pair for a total of 40 layered squares. Cut the squares once diagonally and chain-piece the resulting triangle pairs to make 80 half-square triangle units.

2. Piece 20 Block A as shown above.

3. Make : Layer the 7¼"-wide brown strips and the 7¼"-wide beige leaf strips, right sides together, to make 4 contrasting strip pairs. Cut 4 squares, 7¼" x 7¼", from each strip pair for a total of 16 layered squares. Cut the squares once diagonally and chain-piece the resulting triangle pairs to make 32 half-square triangle units.

4. Cut the half-square triangle units you made in step 3 once diagonally as shown; join the resulting pieces to make 32 Block B as shown above. One unit will be extra.

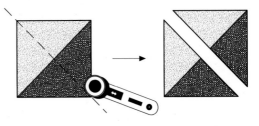

5. Make : Layer the 3⅞"-wide red strips and 2 of the 3⅞"-wide ivory strips, right sides together, to make 2 contrasting strip pairs. Cut 10 squares, 3⅞" x 3⅞", from each strip pair for a total of 20 layered squares. Cut the squares once diagonally and chain-piece the resulting triangle pairs to make 40 half-square triangle units.

6. Make 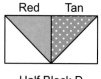: Layer the 3⅞"-wide tan strips and the remaining 3⅞"-wide ivory strips, right sides together, to make 2 contrasting strip pairs. Cut 10 squares, 3⅞" x 3⅞", from each strip pair for a total of 20 layered squares. Cut the squares once diagonally and chain-piece the resulting triangle pairs to make 40 half-square triangle units.

7. Piece 12 Block C as shown on page 93. Then piece 10 Half Block D and 4 Half Block E as shown. You will have 2 ivory/red units and 2 ivory/tan units left over for the quarter blocks used in the quilt corners.

Half Block D
Make 10

Half Block E
Make 4

8. Join the 7¼" brown quarter-square triangles and the 3⅞" beige leaf half-square triangles to make 18 Half Block F as shown.

Half Block F
Make 18

9. Set the blocks and the half and quarter blocks together in rows as shown in the quilt photo; join the rows.

10. Add the dark red inner border and tan plaid outer border as shown in the quilt photo, seaming the dark red strips as necessary. See "Borders with Straight-Cut Corners" on page 100.

11. Layer with batting and backing; quilt or tie. See page 118 for a quilting suggestion. Bind with straight-grain or bias strips of fabric.

Finishing Your Quilt

This section begins with basic information on squaring up blocks and joining them in either straight or on-point (diagonal) sets, and continues with an in-depth discussion of other finishing techniques: adding borders, marking the quilting lines, preparing backing and batting, layering the quilt, quilting and tying, binding, and adding sleeves and labels. A variety of finishing approaches has been used in the quilts included in this book; the photos are an excellent source of ideas.

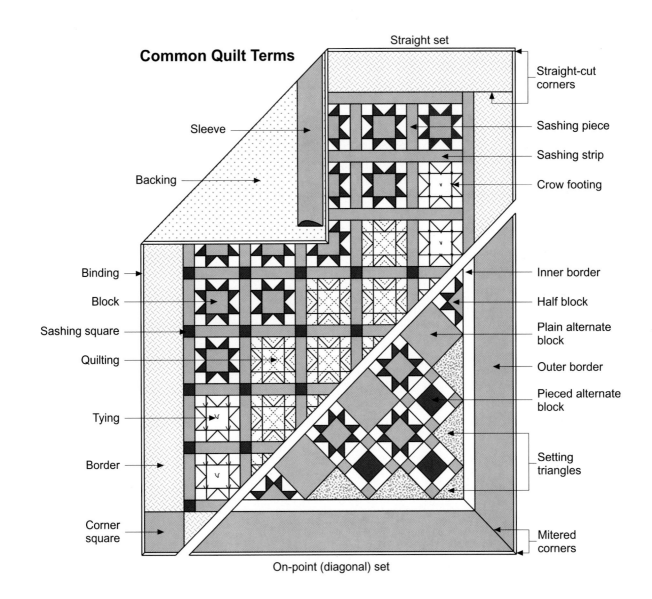

Common Quilt Terms

Straight set

Straight-cut corners

Sashing piece

Sashing strip

Crow footing

Sleeve

Backing

Binding

Block

Sashing square

Quilting

Tying

Border

Corner square

Inner border

Half block

Plain alternate block

Outer border

Pieced alternate block

Setting triangles

Mitered corners

On-point (diagonal) set

Squaring Up Blocks

Some quiltmakers find it necessary to trim or square up their blocks before they assemble them into a quilt top. If you trim, be sure to leave ¼"-wide seam allowances beyond any points or other important block details that fall at the outside edges of the block.

If your block is distorted and doesn't look square, square it up. To do so, cut a piece of plastic-coated freezer paper to the proper size (finished block size plus seam allowance); iron the freezer paper to your ironing board cover, plastic side down. Align the block edges with the edges of the freezer-paper guide and pin. Gently steam press, then cool. Unpin and peel the block away from the paper.

Straight Sets

In straight sets, blocks are laid out in rows that are parallel to the edges of the quilt. Constructing a straight-set quilt is simple and straightforward. When you set blocks side by side without sashing, simply stitch them together in rows. Then, join the rows to complete the patterned section of the quilt. If you are using alternate blocks, cut or piece them to the same size as the primary blocks (including seam allowances), then lay out the primary and alternate blocks in checkerboard fashion and stitch them together in rows.

When setting blocks together with plain sashing, cut the vertical sashing pieces to the same length as the blocks (including seam allowances) and to whatever width you have determined is appropriate. Join the sashing pieces and the blocks to form rows, starting and ending each row with a block. Then, join the rows with long strips of the sashing fabric, cut to the same width as the shorter sashing pieces. Make sure the corners of the blocks are aligned when you stitch the rows together. Add the side sashing strips last.

If your sashing includes corner squares of a color different from the rest of the sashing (sashing squares), cut the vertical sashing pieces and join them to the blocks to form rows, starting and ending each row with a sashing piece. Cut the hori-

zontal sashing pieces the same size as the vertical pieces. Cut sashing squares to the same dimensions as the width of the sashing pieces and join them to the horizontal sashing pieces to make sashing strips. Start and end each row with a sashing square. Join the rows of blocks with these pieced sashing strips.

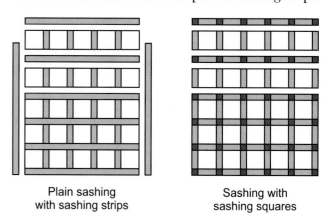

Plain sashing
with sashing strips

Sashing with
sashing squares

On-Point Sets

Quilts that are set on point are constructed in diagonal rows, with half blocks and quarter blocks or setting triangles added to complete the corners and sides of the quilt. If you are designing your own quilt and have no photo or assembly diagram for reference, sketch the quilt on a piece of graph paper so you can see how the rows will go together and how many setting pieces you will need.

Plain setting triangles can be quick-cut from squares. You will always need four corner triangles. To maintain straight grain on the outside edges of the quilt, use half-square triangles. Two squares cut to the proper dimensions and divided once on the diagonal will yield the four half-square triangles needed for the corners.

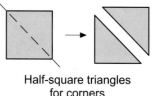

Half-square triangles
for corners

Check your quilt sketch to see how many side triangles are needed. To maintain straight grain on the outside edges, use quarter-square triangles. A square cut to the proper dimensions and divided

twice on the diagonal will yield four quarter-square triangles, so divide the total number of triangles needed by 4, round up to the next whole number, and cut and divide that many squares. In some cases, you will have extra triangles to set aside for another project.

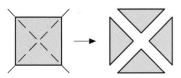

Quarter-square
triangles for sides

How do you determine the "proper dimensions" for cutting these squares? The calculations are based on the finished size of the blocks, and they vary depending on whether the blocks are set side by side or separated by sashing. Though you can use common mathematical formulas (included below) to calculate the cutting dimensions down to a gnat's eyebrow, I prefer the "cut 'em big and trim 'em down" method, which requires mostly simple addition and just one tedious calculation.

The tedious calculation is this: Multiply the finished size of your block by 1.414 to find the *finished diagonal measurement* of the block. You will need this measurement during the planning stage in order to determine the overall size of the patterned section of an on-point quilt and, later, to calculate the cutting dimensions for setting triangles. If the prospect of translating the result of this calculation from decimals to inches is unnerving, just multiply the finished size of your block by 1.5 to get the *approximate finished diagonal measurement* of the block. The result will be accurate enough for the "cut 'em big" approach to setting triangles.

For on-point sets where the blocks are set side by side with no sashing, determine the proper dimensions to cut the squares as follows:

Corners: Add 2½" to the finished measurement of the block. Cut two squares to that size; cut the squares once on the diagonal.

Sides: Calculate the approximate finished diagonal measurement of the block (finished block size x 1.5); add 3" to the result. Cut squares to that size; cut the squares twice on the diagonal. Each square yields four triangles.

For on-point sets where the blocks are separated by sashing, determine the proper dimensions to cut the squares as follows:

Corners: Multiply the finished width of the sashing by 2; add the result to the finished size of the block, then add 2½". Cut two squares to that size; cut the squares once on the diagonal.

Sides: Add the finished width of the sashing to the finished size of the block. Calculate the approximate finished diagonal measurement (block + sash x 1.5); add 3". Cut squares to that size; cut the squares twice on the diagonal. Each square yields four triangles.

These somewhat slapdash calculations will work just fine; exact numbers are unnecessary. If you ever need to know how to calculate cutting dimensions for setting triangles with utter precision, here are the gnat's eyebrow formulas I mentioned above. First, some basic geometry:

When you know the length of the side of a square or right triangle, multiply by 1.414 to get the diagonal measurement.

When you know the length of the diagonal of a square or right triangle, divide by 1.414 to get the side measurement.

For on-point sets where the blocks are set side by side, with no sashing, determine the proper dimensions to cut the squares as follows:

Corners: Divide the finished block size by 1.414. Add .875 (for seams). Round the result up to the nearest ⅛". (Decimal-to-inch conversions are given on page 98.) Cut two squares to that size; cut the squares once on the diagonal.

Sides: Multiply the finished block size by 1.414. Add 1.25 (for seams). Round the result up to the nearest ⅛". Cut squares to that size; cut the squares twice on the diagonal. Each square yields four triangles.

For on-point sets where the blocks are separated by sashing, determine the proper dimensions to cut the squares as follows:

Corners: Multiply the finished width of the sashing by 2. Add the finished block size. Divide the result by 1.414, add .875 (for seams), and round up to the nearest ⅛". (Decimal-to-inch conversions are given below.) Cut two squares to that size; cut the squares once on the diagonal.

Sides: Add the finished width of the sashing to the finished size of the block. Multiply the result by 1.414, add 1.25 (for seams), and round up to the nearest ⅛". Cut squares to that size; cut the squares twice on the diagonal. Each square yields four triangles.

DECIMAL-TO-INCH CONVERSIONS

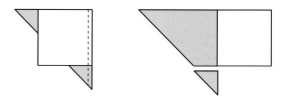

.125	=	⅛"	.625	=	⅝"
.25	=	¼"	.75	=	¾"
.375	=	⅜"	.875	=	⅞"
.50	=	½"			

ASSEMBLING ON-POINT QUILTS

As mentioned in the previous section, quilts laid out with the blocks set on point are constructed in diagonal rows. To avoid confusion, lay out all the blocks and setting pieces in the proper configuration before you start sewing. In an on-point set where blocks are set side by side without sashing, simply pick up and sew one row at a time; then, join the rows.

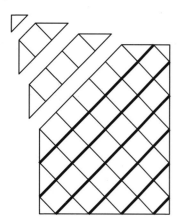

When you use the cut 'em big approach for the setting triangles, the side and corner triangles will be larger than the blocks. Align the square corners of the triangle and the block when you join the

side triangles to the blocks, leaving the excess at the "point" end of the setting triangle. Stitch and press the seam, then trim the excess even with the edge of the block. Attach the corner triangles last, centering the triangles on the blocks so that any excess or shortfall is distributed equally on each side.

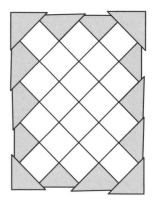

When sewn, your quilt top will look something like this:

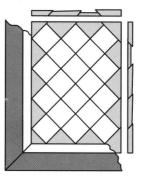

Obviously, you will need to do some trimming and squaring up. At this point, you can make a decision about whether to leave some excess fabric so the blocks will "float" or to trim the setting triangles so that only a ¼"-wide seam allowance remains. Use the outside corners of the blocks to align your cutting guide and trim as desired; make sure the corners are square.

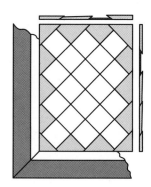

Trimmed to leave ¼" seam allowance (Border, when added, will come to the corners of the blocks.)

Trimmed to allow blocks to float

The assembly order for on-point sets that include sashing is a little more complex. You can see from the drawing below that the side setting triangles span a block plus one sashing strip, and the corner triangles span a block plus two sashing pieces. Before laying out your blocks, sashing pieces, and setting triangles in preparation for sewing, make a photocopy or tracing of your paper quilt plan and slice it into diagonal rows so you can see exactly which pieces constitute a particular row. Once you have joined the pieces into rows, start joining the rows from the bottom right corner and work toward the center. When you reach the center, set that piece aside and go to the top left corner, again working toward the center. Add the top right and bottom left corner triangles last, after the two main sections have been joined.

Add corners last.

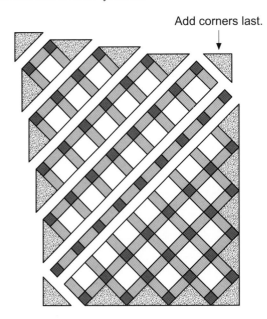

Assembly diagram for on-point set with sashing

Some of us have difficulty getting on-point quilts to lie flat. You can minimize potential problems by taking a few precautions during the cutting and assembly process. Make sure that the individual blocks are absolutely square and are all the same size. Plain or pieced alternate blocks should be perfectly square and exactly the same size as the primary blocks. The 90° corners of the side setting triangles should be truly square. Since these triangles are quick-cut on the bias, sometimes the corners are not square; it's worth taking the time to double-check. When you join blocks to setting triangles, feed them into the sewing machine with the block, which has a straight-grain edge, on top and the bias-edged setting triangle on the bottom.

Bar Quilts

In a bar quilt, various pieced and plain units are joined into rows, or bars, instead of blocks; the pattern emerges only after the bars are stitched together. Several different bar formats may be combined to form the overall pattern of a particular quilt. Make sure the design, fabrics, and colors will come out as you intended by laying out the pieces for several bars—or for the entire quilt—before you start to sew.

For some quilts, bar construction is the only logical method. For many common quilt designs, changing to a bar-quilt approach simplifies construction, reduces the number of seams, and/or creates large seam-free areas in which to quilt. Study a full-quilt photo or a scale drawing of several rows of a quilt to see if old block boundaries can be eliminated and new units of construction identified, as in the examples below.

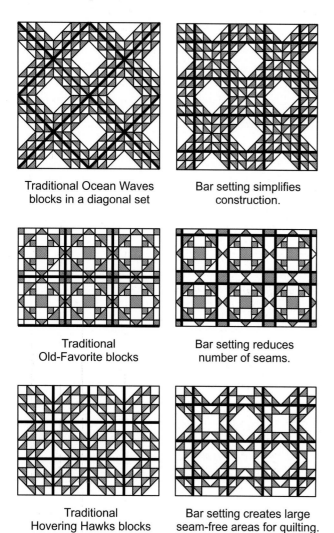

Traditional Ocean Waves blocks in a diagonal set

Bar setting simplifies construction.

Traditional Old-Favorite blocks

Bar setting reduces number of seams.

Traditional Hovering Hawks blocks

Bar setting creates large seam-free areas for quilting.

Borders

Whether or not to add a border to your quilt is entirely up to you. Some quilts seem to resist borders. If you have tried several different border options and none seems to work, perhaps the piece wants to be finished without a border at all or with a border on only one or two sides. Many quilts will happily accept a "1-2-3" border—an inner border, a middle border, and an outer border in 1:2:3 proportions (1" inner, 2" middle, and 3" outer borders, or 1½" inner, 3" middle, and 4½" outer borders, for example).

Though many of us avoid adding elaborately pieced borders to our quilts because of the additional work involved, some quilts demand them. As an alternative, try a multi-fabric border. Use a different fabric on each edge of the quilt; use one fabric for the top and right edges and a different fabric for the bottom and left edges; or, join random chunks of several different fabrics until you have pieces long enough to form borders. Quiltmakers who buy fabric in small cuts often resort to multi-fabric borders out of necessity, as they rarely have enough of any one fabric to border an entire quilt.

Because you need extra yardage to cut borders on the lengthwise grain, plain border strips commonly are cut along the crosswise grain and seamed when extra length is needed. Press these seams open for minimum visibility. To ensure a flat, square quilt, cut border strips extra long and trim the strips to the proper length after you know the actual dimensions of the patterned center section of the quilt.

Most of the quilts in the pattern section of this book have seamed borders with straight-cut corners; a few may have borders with corner squares or with mitered corners.

Straight-cut corners   Corner squares   Mitered corners

BORDERS WITH STRAIGHT-CUT CORNERS

To make a border with straight-cut corners, measure the length of the patterned section of the quilt at the center, from raw edge to raw edge. Cut two border strips to that measurement and join them to the sides of the quilt with a ¼"-wide seam, matching the ends and centers and easing the edges to fit. Then, measure the width of the quilt at the center from edge to edge, including the border pieces that you just added. Cut two border strips to that measurement and join them to the top and bottom of the quilt, matching ends and centers and easing as necessary.

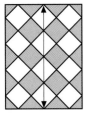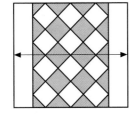

Measure length at center. Measure width at center after adding side borders.

Note: *Do not measure the outer edges of the quilt! Often, these edges measure longer than the quilt center due to stretching during construction; the edges might even be two different lengths. To keep the finished quilt as straight and square as possible, you must measure the centers.*

BORDERS WITH CORNER SQUARES

To make a border with corner squares, measure the length and the width of the patterned section of the quilt at the center, from raw edge to raw edge. Cut two border strips to the lengthwise measurement and join to the sides of the quilt with a $\frac{1}{4}$"-wide seam, matching the ends and centers and easing the edges to fit. Then cut two border strips to the original crosswise measurement, join corner squares to the ends of the strips, and stitch these units to the top and bottom of the quilt, matching ends, seams, and centers and easing as necessary.

BORDERS WITH MITERED CORNERS

To make mitered corners, first estimate the finished outside dimensions of your quilt, including borders. Cut border strips to this length plus at least $\frac{1}{2}$" for seam allowances; it's safer to add 2" to 3" to give yourself some leeway. If your quilt is to have multiple borders, sew the individual strips together and treat the resulting unit as a single piece for mitering.

Mark the centers of the quilt edges and the centers of the border strips. Stitch the borders to the quilt with a $\frac{1}{4}$"-wide seam, matching the centers; the border strip should extend the same distance at each end of the quilt. Start and stop your stitching $\frac{1}{4}$" from the corners of the quilt; press the seams toward the borders.

Lay the first corner to be mitered on the ironing board, pinning as necessary to keep the quilt from pulling and the corner from slipping. Fold one of the border units under at a 45° angle. Work with the fold until seams or stripes meet properly; pin at the fold, then check to see that the outside corner is square and that there is no extra fullness at the edges. When everything is straight and square, press the fold.

Starting at the outside edge of the quilt, center a piece of 1" masking tape over the mitered fold; remove pins as you apply the tape.

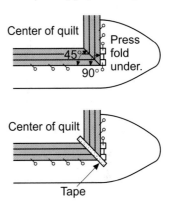

Unpin the quilt from the ironing board and turn it over. Draw a light pencil line on the crease created when you pressed the fold. Fold the center section of the quilt diagonally from the corner, right sides together, and align the long edges of the border strips. Stitch on the pencil line, then remove the tape; trim the excess fabric and press the seam open. Repeat these steps for the remaining three corners.

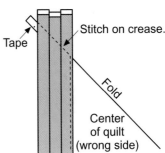

Marking the Quilting Lines

Marking may not be necessary if you are planning to quilt in-the-ditch or to outline-quilt a uniform distance from seam lines. Some quiltmakers do outline quilting "by eye," though many others use ¼"-wide masking tape to mark these lines as they stitch. You can use masking or drafting tape to mark any straight-line quilting design; cut simple shapes from Con-Tact® paper. Apply the tape or adhesive-paper shape when you are ready to quilt and remove promptly after you have quilted along its edge; adhesives left on the quilt too long may leave a residue that is difficult to remove.

Mark more complex quilting designs on the quilt top before layering the quilt with batting and backing. A gridded transparent ruler is useful for measuring and marking straight lines and filler grids. You can place quilting patterns from books or magazines or hand-drawn designs underneath the quilt and trace onto the fabric if the quilt fabrics are fairly light. Use a light box or put your work against a window if you have difficulty seeing the design.

If you cannot see through the quilt fabric, you will have to draw the design directly onto the quilt top. Use a precut plastic stencil, or make your own by drawing or tracing the quilting design on clear plastic; cut out the lines with a double-bladed craft knife, leaving "bridges" every inch or two so the stencil will hold its shape. You can also trace the design onto plain paper (or make a photocopy); cover the paper with one or two layers of clear Con-Tact paper and cut out the lines. Try putting small pieces of double-stick tape on the back of the stencil to keep it in place as you mark the quilting lines.

When marking quilting lines, work on a hard, smooth surface. Use a hard lead pencil (number 3 or 4) on light fabrics; for dark fabrics, try a fine-line chalk marker or a silver, nonphoto blue, or white pencil. Ideally, lines will remain visible for the duration of the quilting process and will be easy to remove when the quilting is done. Light lines are always easier to remove than heavy ones; test to make sure that the lines will wash out after the quilting is completed.

If you are using an allover quilting pattern that does not relate directly to the seams or to a design element of the quilt, you may find it easier to mark the quilting lines on the backing fabric and quilt from the back rather than the front of the quilt.

Backings

The quilt backing should be at least 6" wider and 6" longer than the quilt top. A length of 44"-wide fabric (42 usable inches after preshrinking) is adequate to back a quilt that is no wider than 36". For a larger quilt, buy extra-wide cotton or sew two or more pieces of fabric together. Use a single fabric, seamed as necessary, to make a backing of adequate size, or piece a simple multi-fabric back that complements the front of the quilt. Early quiltmakers often made pieced backings as a matter of necessity; modern quiltmakers see quilt backings as another place to experiment with color and design.

If you opt for a seamed or pieced backing, trim off selvages before you stitch and press seams open.

Calculate the yardage required for single-fabric backings as follows:

For quilts up to 36" wide, any length:
   length + 6"
For quilts 37"–78" wide and no longer than
   78": width + 6" x 2 (1 crosswise seam)
For quilts 37"–78" wide and more than 78"
   long: length + 6" x 2 (1 lengthwise seam)
For quilts more than 78" wide and 79"–120"
   long: width + 6" x 3 (2 crosswise seams)

Batting

Batting comes packaged in standard bed sizes; you can also buy it by the yard. Several weights or thicknesses are available. Thick battings are fine for tied quilts and comforters; choose a thinner batting if you intend to quilt by hand or machine.

Thin batting is available in 100% cotton, 100% polyester, and an 80%/20% cotton/polyester blend. The cotton/polyester blend supposedly combines the best features of the two fibers. All-cotton batting is soft and drapable but requires close quilting and produces quilts that are rather flat. Though many quilters like the antique look, some find cotton batting difficult to "needle." Glazed or bonded polyester batting is sturdy and easy to handle, and it washes well. It requires less quilting than cotton and has more loft. However, polyester fibers sometimes migrate through fabric, creating tiny white "beards" on the surface of a quilt. The dark gray and black polyester battings now available can ease this problem for quiltmakers who like to work with dark fabrics; bearding is less noticeable.

Unroll your batting and let it "relax" overnight before you layer your quilt. Some battings may need to be prewashed, while others should definitely not be prewashed; be sure to check the manufacturer's instructions.

Layering the Quilt

Once you have marked your quilt top, pieced and pressed your backing, and let your batting relax, you are ready to layer the quilt. Spread the backing, wrong side up, on a flat, clean surface; anchor it with pins or masking tape. Spread the batting over the backing, smoothing out any wrinkles; then, center the quilt top on the back-

ing, right side up. Be careful not to stretch or distort any of the layers as you work. Starting in the middle, pin-baste the three layers together, gently smoothing any fullness to the sides and corners.

Now, baste the three layers together with a long needle and light-colored thread; start in the center and work diagonally to each corner, making a large **X**. Continue basting, laying in a grid of horizontal and vertical lines 6" to 8" apart. Finish by basting around the outside edges.

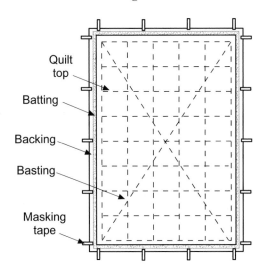

Quilt
top

Batting

Backing

Basting

Masking
tape

Quilting

The purpose of quilting or tying is to keep the three layers together and to prevent the batting from lumping or shifting. Quilts typically are tied with knots either on the front or the back, or they are machine or hand quilted. Quiet exploration is taking place in this facet of quiltmaking. While several old methods for tying and quilting are being revived, some quiltmakers are stretching tradition by "tying" with eyelets or decorative studs or quilting with unusual materials, including narrow ribbon, wire, and even cassette tape.

MACHINE QUILTING

Machine quilting is suitable for all types of quilts, from simple baby and bed quilts that will be washed frequently to sophisticated pieces for the wall. With machine quilting, you can quickly complete quilts that might otherwise languish on the shelf. The technique provides some creative challenges as well.

Unless you plan to stitch in-the-ditch, mark the quilting lines before you layer the quilt. Consider using a simple allover grid or a continuous-line quilting design. Basting for machine quilting is usually done with safety pins; if you have a large work surface to support the quilt and an even-feed foot for your sewing machine, you should have no problem with shifting layers or untidy pleats, tucks, and bubbles on the back side. Remove the safety pins as you sew. Pull thread ends to the back and work them into the quilt for a more professional look.

Try machine quilting with threads of unusual types and weights or experiment with the decorative stitch or twin-needle capabilities of your sewing machine. Double-needle quilting produces an interesting, corded effect.

TRADITIONAL HAND QUILTING

To quilt by hand, you will need short, sturdy needles (called "Betweens"), quilting thread, and a thimble to fit the middle finger of your sewing hand. Most quilters also use a frame or hoop to support their work. Quilting needles run from size 3 to 12; the higher the number, the smaller the needle. Use the smallest needle you can comfortably handle; the smaller the needle, the smaller your stitches.

Thread your needle with a single strand of quilting thread about 18" long; make a small knot and insert the needle in the top layer about 1" from the place where you want to start stitching. Pull the needle out at the point where quilting will begin and gently pull the thread until the knot pops through the fabric and into the batting.

Begin your quilting line with a backstitch and continue with a small, even running stitch. Place your left hand underneath the quilt so you can feel the needle point with the tip of a finger when you take a stitch.

Push the needle through all the layers with the thimble on your middle finger of your "top hand," using the dimples in the side or end of the thimble (whichever is more comfortable) to support the eye end of the needle. When you feel the tip of the needle with the middle or index finger of the "underneath" hand, simultaneously rock the needle eye down toward the quilt surface, depress the fabric in front of the needle with the thumb of the top hand, and push the needle tip up with the underneath finger.

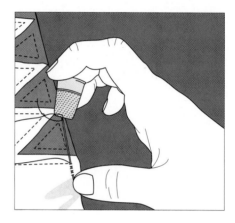

When the needle tip comes through to the top of the quilt, relax the top-hand thumb and the underneath finger, rock the needle eye up so it is almost perpendicular to the quilt, and push the needle through the layers to start the next stitch. Repeat the process until you have three or four stitches on the needle, then pull the needle all the way through, taking up any slack in the thread, and start again.

To end a line of quilting, make a small knot close to the last stitch; then, backstitch, running the thread a needle's length through the batting. Gently pull the thread until the knot pops into the batting; clip the thread at the quilt's surface. Remove basting stitches as you quilt, leaving only those that go around the outside edges of the quilt.

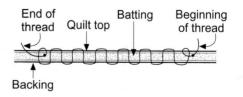

End of thread   Quilt top   Batting   Beginning of thread

Backing

UTILITY QUILTING

Utility quilting is faster than traditional hand quilting but "homier" than machine quilting; you use big needles and heavy threads (like perle cotton, crochet thread, or several strands of embroidery floss) and take big stitches, anywhere from 1/8" to 1/4" in length. The method is well worth considering for casual, scrappy quilts and for pieces you might otherwise plan to machine quilt. Quilts finished with this technique are unquestionably sturdy; the added surface texture is very pleasing.

You can do utility quilting freehand, without marking the quilt top, or mark quilting lines as usual. Use the shortest, finest, sharp-pointed needle you can get the thread through; try several different kinds to find the needle that works best for you. I like working with #8 perle cotton and a #6 Between needle. Keep your stitches as straight and even as possible.

Crow Footing and Other Tacking Techniques

I have an old comforter in my collection that is tied with a technique called "crow footing." Crow footing is done with a long needle and thick thread, such as a single or double strand of perle cotton or crochet thread. Isolated fly stitches are worked in a grid across the surface of the quilt, leaving a small diagonal stitch on the back of the quilt; there are no visible knots or dangling threads. Stitches can be spaced as far apart as the length of your needle will allow.

Put your work in a hoop or frame. Use a long, sharp-pointed needle—try Cotton Darners, millinery needles, or soft-sculpture needles. Make a small knot in the thread and insert the needle in the top layer of the quilt about 1" from A. Pull the needle out at A and gently pull the thread until the knot pops through the fabric and into the batting. Hold the thread down with the thumb and insert the needle at B as shown; go *through all three layers* and bring the needle out at C. Insert the needle at D

and travel *through the top layer only* to start the next stitch at A.

Work in rows from the top to the bottom or from the right to the left of the quilt, spacing the stitches 2" to 3" apart. To end stitching, bring the needle out at C and make a small knot about 1/8" from the surface of the quilt. Make a backstitch at D, running the thread through the batting an inch or so; pop the knot into the batting and clip the thread at the surface of the quilt.

Crow Footing

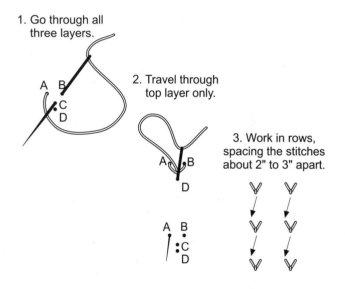

1. Go through all three layers.

2. Travel through top layer only.

3. Work in rows, spacing the stitches about 2" to 3" apart.

OTHER TACKING TECHNIQUES

Backstitch tacking is another option. Two favorite stitches are the Mennonite tack and the Methodist knot. Both stitches are best worked from the right to the left rather than from the top to the bottom of the quilt; they leave a small horizontal stitch on the back of the quilt.

To do the Mennonite Tack, bring the needle out at A and take a backstitch 1/4" to 3/8" long *through all three layers*, coming back up just a few threads from the starting point (B–C). Reinsert the needle at D and travel *through the top layer only* to start the next stitch. The tiny second stitch, which should be almost invisible, crosses over the backstitch and locks the tacking.

Mennonite Tack

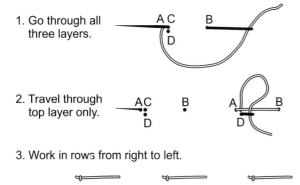

1. Go through all three layers.

2. Travel through top layer only.

3. Work in rows from right to left.

The Methodist knot is done with two loose backstitches. Bring the needle out at A and take a backstitch through all three layers, coming back up beyond the starting point (B–C). Reinsert the needle at A and travel through the top layer only to start the next stitch.

Methodist Knot

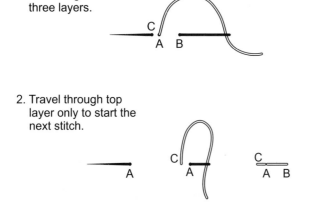

1. Go through all three layers.

2. Travel through top layer only to start the next stitch.

You can lay in any of these tacking stitches at random, rather than on a uniform grid. Early quiltmakers who used these techniques often worked with the quilt stretched full size on a large floor frame, working from both ends and rolling in the edges of the quilt as the rows of tacking were completed, thus eliminating the need for basting. You can tie or tack small quilts without basting if you spread the layers smoothly over a table or other large, flat work surface.

Binding

When the tying or quilting is complete, prepare for binding your quilt by removing any remaining basting threads, except for the stitches around the outside edges of the quilt. Trim the batting and backing even with the edges of the quilt top. Use a rotary cutter and cutting guide to get accurate, straight edges; make sure the corners are square.

Make enough binding to go around the perimeter of the quilt, plus about 18". The general instructions below are based on ³/₈"-wide (finished), double-fold binding, which is made from strips cut 2¹/₂" wide and stitched to the outside edges of the quilt with a ³/₈"-wide seam. Cutting dimensions and seam widths for bindings in other sizes are given in the chart on page 109.

Straight-grain binding is fine for most applications. Simply cut strips from the lengthwise or crosswise grain of the fabric; one crosswise strip will yield about 40" of binding. For ³/₈"-wide (finished) binding, cut the strips 2¹/₂" wide. Trim the ends of the strips at a 45° angle and seam the ends to make a long, continuous strip; press seam allowances open.

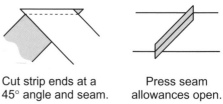

Cut strip ends at a 45° angle and seam.   Press seam allowances open.

Fold the strip in half lengthwise, wrong sides together, and press.

Use bias binding if your quilt edges have curves or if you expect the quilt to get heavy use; binding cut on the bias does wear longer. Some quilters cut bias strips from a flat piece of fabric, joining the strips after cutting; others prefer the tubular method for making a continuous bias strip.

To make flat-cut binding, lay out a length of fabric. (Fabric requirements are given on page 107.) Make a bias cut, starting at one corner of the fabric; use the 45° marking on a long cutting ruler as a guide. Then, cut bias strips, measuring from the edges of the initial bias cut. For ³/₈"-wide (finished) binding, cut the strips 2½" wide. Seam the ends to make a long, continuous strip; press seams open. Fold the strip in half lengthwise, wrong sides together, and press.

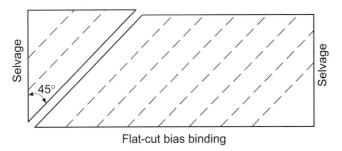

Flat-cut bias binding

For ³/₈"-wide (finished) binding made from 2½"-wide strips:

¼ yard fabric yields about 115" of binding
³/₈ yard fabric yields about 180" of binding
½ yard fabric yields about 255" of binding
⅝ yard fabric yields about 320" of binding
¾ yard fabric yields about 400" of binding
⅞ yard fabric yields about 465" of binding

Continuous bias binding can be made from a square of fabric. To determine what size square will yield the amount of bias binding you need, multiply the length of bias needed (in inches) by the width you plan to cut it, then use a pocket calculator to find the square root of the result.

Let's say you are planning to finish a 72" x 84" quilt with ³/₈"-wide finished binding, which requires 2½"-wide strips. You will need 330" of binding (quilt perimeter plus 18"); 330 x 2½ = 825. The square root of 825 is 28.72. Thus, a 29" to 30" square will yield the 330" of binding you need.

Remove the selvage and mark the top and bottom of the square with pins. Divide the square on the diagonal to make two half-square triangles.

Mark top and bottom of square and divide it on the diagonal.

With right sides together, join the marked sides of the triangles with a ¼" seam; press seam open.

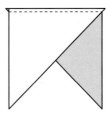

Join the marked sides.

Measure and draw lines the width of the binding strips on the wrong side of the fabric, starting at one of the long, bias edges as shown in the drawing below. If the distance between the last line and the bottom edge is less than the strip width you need, trim to the line above. Slice along the top and bottom lines (at the ends closest to the seam) for a distance of about 6" as shown.

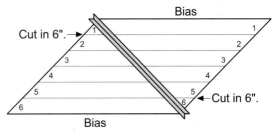

Draw lines on wrong side of fabric. Slice in 6" along top and bottom lines.

With right sides together and the *edges offset by the width of one line*, stitch the ends together to form a cylinder; press seam open. Starting at the top, cut along the marked lines to form a continuous bias strip. Fold the strip in half lengthwise, wrong sides together, and press.

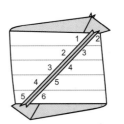

Stitch ends together to form a cylinder, offsetting edges by width of one line.

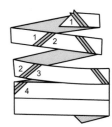

Cut along lines to form a continuous strip.

Two different methods of applying the binding to the quilt are described below. One produces a binding with mitered corners, with the binding applied in a continuous strip around the edges of the quilt. In the second method, measured lengths of binding are applied separately to each edge of the quilt. In both cases, the instructions given are based on ³/₈"-wide finished binding; you will need to use a different seam width if your finished binding is narrower or wider than ³/₈".

BINDINGS WITH MITERED CORNERS

For a binding with mitered corners, start near the center of one side of the quilt. Place the binding on the front of the quilt, lining up the raw edges of the binding with the raw edges of the quilt. Using an even-feed foot, sew the binding to the quilt with a ³/₈"-wide seam; leave the first 8" to 10" of binding loose so that you can join or overlap the beginning and ending of the binding strip later. Be careful not to stretch the quilt or the binding as you sew. When you reach the corner, stop the stitching ³/₈" from the edge of the quilt and backstitch; clip threads.

Turn the quilt to prepare for sewing along the next edge. Fold the binding up and away; then, fold it again to bring it along the edge of the quilt. There will be an angled fold at the corner; the straight fold should be even with the top edge of the quilt.

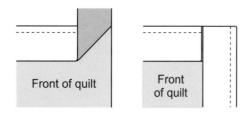

Stitch from the straight fold in the binding to the next corner, pinning as necessary to keep the binding lined up with the raw edge of the quilt. When you reach the next corner, stop the stitching ³/₈" from the edge of the quilt and backstitch; clip threads. Fold the binding as you did at the last corner and continue around the edge of the quilt.

Stop and backstitch about 12" from the starting point. Overlap the end of the remaining unattached binding and the tail you left when you started and adjust them to fit the quilt exactly. Join with a diagonal seam; trim the excess. Stitch this newly joined section to the quilt.

Fold the binding to the back, over the raw edges of the quilt; the folded edge of the binding should just cover the machine-stitching line. Blindstitch the binding in place, making sure your stitches do not go through to the front of the quilt. At the corners, fold the binding to form miters on the front and back of the quilt; stitch down the folds in the miters.

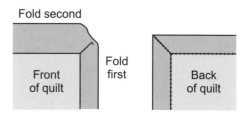

BINDINGS WITH MEASURED STRIPS

Use this binding method if the outside edges of your quilt need to be eased to the binding so that their finished measurements conform to the quilt's center measurements. Straight-grain binding strips work best for this type of binding.

Bind the long edges of the quilt first. Measure the length of the quilt at the center, raw edge to raw edge.

Note: *Do not measure the outer edges of the quilt. Often the edges measure longer than the quilt center due to stretching during construction; the edges might even be two different lengths.*

From your long strip of binding, cut two pieces of binding to the lengthwise center measurement. Working from the right side of the quilt, pin the binding strips to the long edges of the quilt, matching the ends and centers and easing the edges to fit as necessary. Use an even-feed foot and sew the binding to the quilt with a ³/₈"-wide seam. Fold the binding to the back, over the raw edges of the quilt; the folded edge of the binding should just cover the machine-stitching line. Blindstitch the binding in place, making sure your stitches do not go through to the front of the quilt.

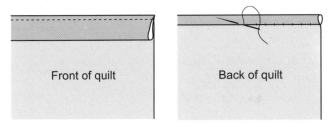

Front of quilt

Back of quilt

Now measure the width of the quilt at the center, outside edge to outside edge. From the remainder of your long binding strip, cut two pieces to that measurement plus 1". Pin these measured binding strips to the short edges of the quilt, matching the centers and leaving ½" of the binding extending at each end; ease the edges to fit as necessary. Sew the binding to the quilt with a ³/₈"-wide seam.

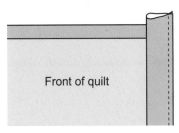

Front of quilt

To finish, fold the extended portion of the binding strips down over the bound edges; then, bring the binding to the back and blindstitch in place as before.

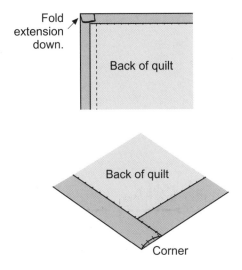

Fold extension down.

Back of quilt

Back of quilt

Corner

Strip and seam widths for double-fold bindings in various finished sizes are as follows:

Binding	Strip Width	Seam
¼"	1¾"	¼"
³/₈"	2½"	³/₈"
½"	3¼"	½"
⅝"	4"	⅝"
¾"	4¾"	¾"

Sleeves and Labels

Quilts that will be displayed on walls should have a sleeve tacked to the back near the top edge, to hold a hanging rod. I put sleeves on all my quilts, even those intended for beds, so they can be safely hung if they are suddenly requested for an exhibit or if their owners decide to use them for decoration rather than as bedding.

Sleeves should be a generous width. Use a piece of fabric 6" to 8" wide and 1" to 2" shorter than the finished width of the quilt at the top edge. Hem the ends. Then, fold the fabric strip in half lengthwise, wrong sides together; seam the long, raw edges together with a ¼" seam. Fold the tube so that the seam is centered on one side and press the seam allowances open.

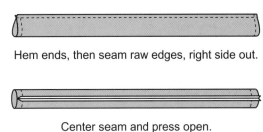

Hem ends, then seam raw edges, right side out.

Center seam and press open.

Place the tube on the back side of the quilt, just under the top binding, with the seamed side against the quilt. Hand sew the top edge of the sleeve to the quilt, taking care not to catch the front of the quilt as you stitch.

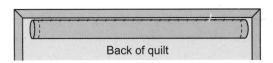

Back of quilt

Tack down top edge of sleeve.

Push the front side of the tube up so the top edge covers about half of the binding (providing a little "give" so the hanging rod does not put strain on the quilt itself) and sew the bottom edge of the sleeve in place as shown.

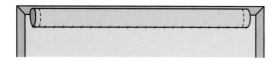

Push tube up and tack down bottom edge.

Slide a curtain rod, a wooden dowel, or a piece of lath through the sleeve. The seamed side of the sleeve will keep the rod from coming into direct contact with the quilt. Suspend the rod on brackets. Or, attach screw eyes or drill holes at each end of the rod and slip the holes or eyes over small nails.

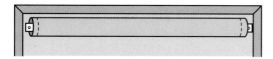

Insert hanging rod in sleeve.

Be sure to sign and date your work! At the very least, embroider your name and the year you completed the quilt on the front or back of the quilt. Quilt historians and the future owners of your quilts will want to know more than just the "who" and "when." Consider tacking a handwritten or typed label to the back of the quilt that includes the name of the quilt, your name, your city and state, the date, whom you made the quilt for and why, and any other interesting or important information about the quilt.

Press a piece of plastic-coated freezer paper to the wrong side of the label fabric to stabilize it while you write or type. For a handwritten label, use a permanent marking pen; use a multistrike ribbon for typewritten labels. Always test to be absolutely sure the ink is permanent!

Note: *Hand- or typewritten labels that pass the washing-machine test sometimes run and bleed when they are dry-cleaned.*

Quilting Suggestions

Each diagram represents one block unless otherwise noted.

ANVIL STAR
(page 18)

4 blocks

STATE FAIR
(page 22)

2 blocks

SHADED PINWHEEL
(page 20)

SNOWBALL STRIP
(page 25)

4 blocks

ARMY STAR
(page 28)

4 blocks

HARMONY SQUARE
(page 33)

SQUARES AND LADDERS
(page 30)

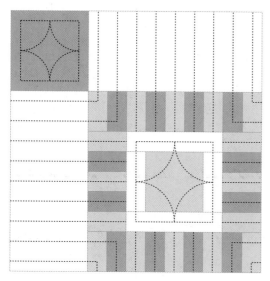

Corner of quilt

HOMEWARD BOUND TO UNION SQUARE
(page 36)

4 blocks

BEAR'S PAW
(page 39)

GAGGLE OF GEESE
(page 44)

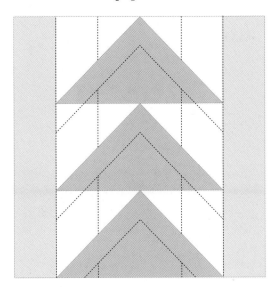

STRING SQUARE
(page 42)

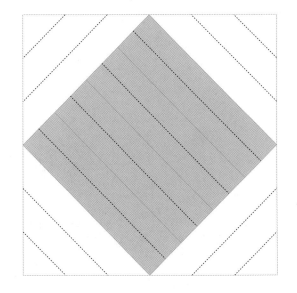

THE COMET
(page 46)

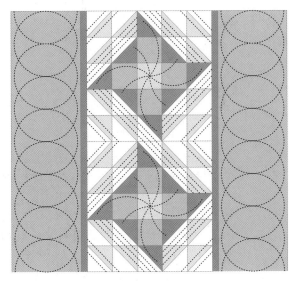

Corner of quilt

CHRISTMAS STAR
(page 48)

SQUARES AND POINTS
(page 52)

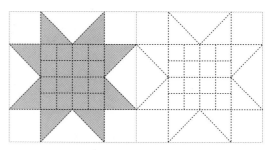

1 pieced and 1 alternate block

LONDON ROADS
(page 50)

Corner of quilt

ROLLING PINWHEEL
(page 55)

NINEPATCH PLAID
(page 58)

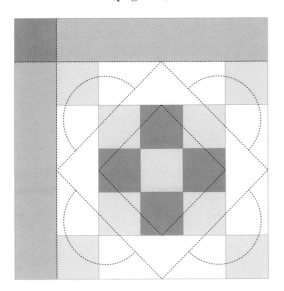

SPLIT NINEPATCH
(page 64)

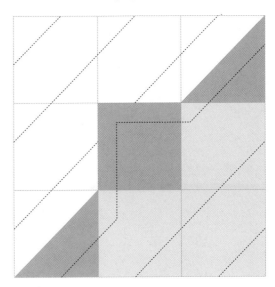

HOLLY'S HOUSES
(page 61)

FLYING BIRDS
(page 67)

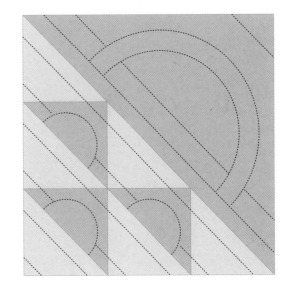

DOUBLE SQUARES
(page 70)

GENTLEMAN'S FANCY
(page 74)

LOUISIANA
(page 72)

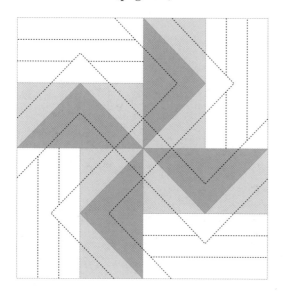

BROKEN WHEEL
(page 76)

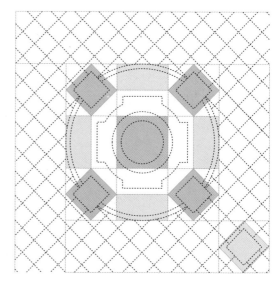

Corner of quilt

SUMMER WINDS
(page 79)

A BRIGHTER DAY
(page 85)

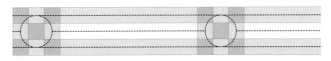

1 row

FOUR-FOUR TIME
(page 82)

OREGON TRAIL
(page 88)

LADY OF THE LAKE
(page 90)

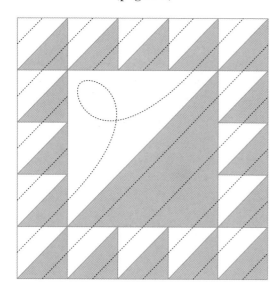

PINWHEEL MOSAIC
(page 92)

Corner of quilt

Meet the Author

Lasting Impressions Photography Studio

Judy Hopkins is a prolific quiltmaker whose fondness for traditional design goes hand in hand with an unwavering commitment to fast, contemporary cutting and piecing techniques. Judy has been making quilts since 1980 and working full-time at the craft since 1985. Her work has been seen in numerous exhibits and publications.

Writing and teaching are by-products of Judy's intense involvement in the process of creating quilts. She is the author of *Four-Patch Blocks & Quilts for the ScrapSaver*, *Five- and Seven-Patch Blocks & Quilts for the ScrapSaver*, *Nine-Patch Blocks & Quilts for the ScrapSaver*, *One-of-a-Kind Quilts*, *Fit To Be Tied*, and *Around the Block with Judy Hopkins*, and co-author (with Nancy J. Martin) of *Rotary Riot* and *Rotary Roundup*. For the last several years, Judy

has been working primarily from the scrap bag. Faced with a daunting accumulation of scraps and limited time to deal with them, she started looking for ways to apply quick-cutting methods to scrap fabrics. This led to the design of Judy's popular ScrapMaster ruler (formerly the ScrapSaver), a tool for quick-cutting half-square triangles from irregularly shaped scraps, and the accompanying series of books.

Judy lives in Anchorage, Alaska, with her husband, Bill, and their Labrador retriever, Buckshot Ricochet. She has two grown daughters and two adorable and brilliant grandchildren, who like to help her sew. Judy is active in her local guild, the Anchorage Log Cabin Quilters, and teaches regularly at Calicoes and Quilts Unlimited.

That Patchwork Place Publications and Products

All the Blocks Are Geese • Mary Sue Suit
All New Copy Art for Quilters
All-Star Sampler • Roxanne Carter
Angle Antics • Mary Hickey
Animas Quilts • Jackie Robinson
Appliqué Borders • Jeana Kimball
Appliqué in Bloom • Gabrielle Swain
Appliquilt® • Tonee White
Appliquilt® for Christmas • Tonee White
Appliquilt® Your ABCs • Tonee White
Around the Block with Judy Hopkins
Baltimore Bouquets • Mimi Dietrich
Bargello Quilts • Marge Edie
Basic Beauties • Eileen Westfall
Bias Square® Miniatures • Christine Carlson
Biblical Blocks • Rosemary Makhan
Blockbender Quilts • Margaret J. Miller
Block by Block • Beth Donaldson
Borders by Design • Paulette Peters
Botanical Wreaths • Laura M. Reinstatler
The Calico House • Joanna Brazier
The Cat's Meow • Janet Kime
Celebrate! with Little Quilts • Alice Berg,
    Sylvia Johnson & Mary Ellen Von Holt
A Child's Garden of Quilts • Christal Carter
Colourwash Quilts • Deirdre Amsden
Corners in the Cabin • Paulette Peters
Country Medallion Sampler • Carol Doak
Country Threads
    • Connie Tesene & Mary Tendall
Decoupage Quilts • Barbara Roberts
Designing Quilts • Suzanne Hammond
Down the Rotary Road with Judy Hopkins
The Easy Art of Appliqué
    • Mimi Dietrich & Roxi Eppler
Easy Machine Paper Piecing • Carol Doak
Easy Mix & Match Machine Paper
    Piecing • Carol Doak
Easy Paper-Pieced Keepsake Quilts
    • Carol Doak
Easy Quilts...By Jupiter!® • Mary Beth Maison
Easy Reversible Vests • Carol Doak
Fantasy Flowers • Doreen Cronkite Burbank
Five- and Seven-Patch Blocks & Quilts
    for the ScrapSaver • Judy Hopkins
Four-Patch Blocks & Quilts for the
    ScrapSaver • Judy Hopkins
Freedom in Design • Mia Rozmyn
Fun with Fat Quarters • Nancy J. Martin
Go Wild with Quilts • Margaret Rolfe
Go Wild with Quilts—Again! • Margaret Rolfe

Great Expectations • Karey Bresenhan
    with Alice Kish & Gay E. McFarland
Happy Endings • Mimi Dietrich
The Heirloom Quilt
    • Yolande Filson & Roberta Przybylski
In The Beginning • Sharon Evans Yenter
Irma's Sampler • Irma Eskes
Jacket Jazz • Judy Murrah
Jacket Jazz Encore • Judy Murrah
The Joy of Quilting
    • Joan Hanson & Mary Hickey
Le Rouvray • Diane de Obaldia with Marie-
    Christine Flocard & Cosabeth Parriaud
Little Quilts • Alice Berg, Sylvia Johnson &
    Mary Ellen Von Holt
Lively Little Logs • Donna McConnell
Loving Stitches • Jeana Kimball
Machine Quilting Made Easy • Maurine Noble
Make Room for Quilts • Nancy J. Martin
Mirror Manipulations • Gail Valentine
Nifty Ninepatches • Carolann M. Palmer
Nine-Patch Blocks & Quilts for the
    ScrapSaver • Judy Hopkins
Not Just Quilts • Jo Parrott
Oh! Christmas Trees
On to Square Two • Marsha McCloskey
Osage County Quilt Factory
    • Virginia Robertson
Our Pieceful Village • Lynn Rice
Patchwork Basics • Marie-Christine Flocard
    & Cosabeth Parriaud
A Perfect Match • Donna Lynn Thomas
Picture Perfect Patchwork • Naomi Norman
A Pioneer Doll and Her Quilts • Mary Hickey
Pioneer Storybook Quilts • Mary Hickey
Prairie People—Cloth Dolls to Make and
    Cherish • Marji Hadley & J. Dianne Ridgley
Quick & Easy Quiltmaking • Mary Hickey,
    Nancy J. Martin, Marsha McCloskey &
    Sara Nephew
The Quilt Patch • Leslie Anne Pfeifer
The Quilt Room
    • Pam Lintott & Rosemary Miller
The Quilted Apple • Laurene Sinema
Quilted for Christmas
Quilted for Christmas, Book II
Quilted Legends of the West
    • Judy Zehner & Kim Mosher
Quilted Sea Tapestries • Ginny Eckley
The Quilters' Companion
The Quilting Bee • Jackie Wolff & Lori Aluna
Quilting Makes the Quilt • Lee Cleland

Quilts for All Seasons • Christal Carter
Quilts for Baby • Ursula Reikes
Quilts for Kids • Carolann M. Palmer
Quilts for Red-Letter Days • Janet Kime
Quilts from Nature • Joan Colvin
Quilts from the Smithsonian • Mimi Dietrich
Quilts to Share • Janet Kime
Refrigerator Art Quilts • Jennifer Paulson
Repiecing the Past • Sara Rhodes Dillow
Rotary Riot • Judy Hopkins & Nancy J. Martin
Rotary Roundup
    • Judy Hopkins & Nancy J. Martin
Round About Quilts • J. Michelle Watts
Round Robin Quilts
    • Pat Magaret & Donna Slusser
ScrapMania • Sally Schneider
Seasoned with Quilts • Retta Warehime
Sensational Settings • Joan Hanson
Shortcuts: A Concise Guide to Rotary
    Cutting • Donna Lynn Thomas
Shortcuts Sampler • Roxanne Carter
Shortcuts to the Top • Donna Lynn Thomas
Simply Scrappy Quilts • Nancy J. Martin
Small Talk • Donna Lynn Thomas
Smoothstitch® Quilts • Roxi Eppler
Square Dance • Martha Thompson
The Stitchin' Post • Jean Wells & Lawry Thorn
Stringing Along with Vanessa-Ann
    • Trice Boerens
Stripples • Donna Lynn Thomas
Sunbonnet Sue All Through the Year
    • Sue Linker
Tea Party Time • Nancy J. Martin
Template-Free® Quiltmaking • Trudie Hughes
Template-Free® Quilts and Borders
    • Trudie Hughes
Template-Free® Stars • Jo Parrott
Through the Window & Beyond
    • Lynne Edwards
Treasures from Yesteryear, Book One
    • Sharon Newman
Treasures from Yesteryear, Book Two
    • Sharon Newman
Trouble Free Triangles • Gayle Bong
Two for Your Money • Jo Parrott
Watercolor Impressions
    • Pat Magaret & Donna Slusser
Watercolor Quilts
    • Pat Magaret & Donna Slusser
Woven & Quilted • Mary Anne Caplinger
WOW! Wool-on-Wool Folk Art Quilts
    • Janet Carija Brandt

4", 6", 8", & metric Bias Square® • BiRangle™ • Ruby Beholder™ • ScrapMaster • Rotary Rule™ • Rotary Mate™ • Bias Stripper™
Shortcuts to America's Best-Loved Quilts (video)

Many titles are available at your local quilt shop. For more information, send $2 for a color catalog to
That Patchwork Place, Inc., PO Box 118, Bothell WA 98041-0118 USA.

☎ Call 1-800-426-3126 for the name and location of the quilt shop nearest you.